T0214209

AUTONOMIC SYSTEMS

The AUTONOMIC SYSTEMS book series provides a platform of communication between academia and industry by publishing research monographs, outstanding PhD theses, and peer-reviewed compiled contributions on the latest developments in the field of autonomic systems.

It covers a broad range of topics from the theory of autonomic systems that are researched by academia and industry. Hence, cutting-edge research, prototypical case studies, as well as industrial applications are in the focus of this book series. Fast reviewing provides a most convenient way to publish latest results in this rapid moving research area.

The topics covered by the series include (among others):

- self-* properties in autonomic systems (e.g. self-management, self-healing)
- architectures, models, and languages for building autonomic systems
- trust, negotiation, and risk management in autonomic systems
- theoretical foundations of autonomic systems
- applications and novel computing paradigms of autonomic systems

Autonomics Development: A Domain-Specific Aspect Language Approach

Paul Soule

Birkhäuser

Paul Soule
Elmbrook
Patch Elm Lane
Rangeworthy
Bristol, BS37 7LU
United Kingdom

1998 ACM Computing Classification: C.2.4 [Distributed Systems]; D.3 [Programming languages] D.3.2 [Language Classifications]: Distributed Languages; (Very) high-level languages; D.3.4 [Processors]: Code generation; Compilers; D.2.11 [Software Architectures]: Domain-specific architectures; Languages.

2010 Mathematics Subject Classification: 68-02, 68M14, 68N15, 68N19, 68N20

ISBN 978-3-0346-0539-7   e-ISBN 978-3-0346-0540-3
DOI 10.1007/978-3-0346-0540-3

Library of Congress Control Number: 2010929106

Printed on acid-free paper

Springer Basel AG is part of Springer Science+Business Media

www.birkhauser.ch

Contents

Autonomics Development: A Domain-Specific Aspect Language Approach, IX–X
Book Series: Autonomic Systems
© 2010 Springer Basel AG

Preface

Distributed applications are difficult to write. Programmers need to adhere to specific distributed systems programming conventions and frameworks, which makes distributed systems development complex and error prone and ties the resultant application to the distributed system because the application's code is tangled with the crosscutting concern *distribution.*

Existing mainstream programming languages, such as Java, do not provide language support for distribution. Rather, programmers must rely on object-oriented distribution frameworks to provide distribution support. Although highly successful, the cost of using these frameworks is that the resultant code is tied to the framework. Object-oriented frameworks in general, and distribution frameworks in particular, can therefore be considered crosscutting in nature because the framework's code, either via inheritance or containment, is scattered throughout the application's code thereby tying the application to the framework.

This is a particular concern in distributed systems development because distribution frameworks impose a large code overhead due to the requirements distributed systems impose, such as the need to catch distribution-specific exceptions, locating and binding to distributed objects, locating another server in the event the current server becomes unavailable, and adhering to programming conventions dictated by the framework, such as implementing framework specific interfaces. Consequently, developing distributed applications is complex and error prone and results in application components tied to the distribution framework, which cannot be easily reused outside the application.

In this book we address the above issues and present four contributions to distributed systems development. Firstly, we introduce the concept of a *Distribution Definition Language,* a high-level domain-specific aspect language that generalises the distribution concern by describing the classes and methods of an existing application to be made remote, the distributed system to use to make them remote and the recovery mechanism to use in the event of a remote error. Secondly, we provide the ability for multiple distribution protocols to be applied to the same code base thereby generalising the distribution concern. Thirdly, we allow the application of distribution awareness to applications in such a way that the application is oblivious of the distribution implementation and recovery mechanism yet is able to fully participate in both. Finally, we provide a simplified approach to the development of distributed systems that allows an application to be either distributed or non-distributed, thereby improving software reuse and simplifying testability of distributed applications as applications may be functionally tested before having the distribution and recovery concerns applied.

These contributions, by alleviating some of the complexity involved in distributed systems development and by allowing autonomic features, such as recovery, to be transparently added to existing applications, provides a contribution to autonomic computing.

We introduce a software tool in the form of the RemoteJ compiler/generator that uses information contained in the Distribution Definition Language to generate the distributed system specific code and apply it to the application using bytecode manipulation and generation techniques. Finally, we evaluate our contributions and show that the concept of a Distribution Definition Language simplifies the development of distributed applications whilst allowing for greater reuse of application components.

Autonomics Development: A Domain-Specific Aspect Language Approach, 1–6
Book Series: Autonomic Systems
© 2010 Springer Basel AG

1 Introduction

The widespread adoption of the Internet and associated technologies has resulted in a huge increase in the number of distributed systems, both Internet and Intranet facing. Numerous legacy systems have been, or are being, adapted to provide an Internet presence and to integrate to customers' and suppliers' systems. In addition, faster and more reliable networks have greatly contributed to the success of distributed systems.

However, distributed systems development is still based on the decades old concept of the use of object-oriented frameworks or programming libraries. Although highly successful, the cost of using these frameworks or libraries is that the resultant code is tied to the framework as the distribution framework is scattered and tangled throughout the application making reuse of the code in other domains difficult, if not impossible. This introduces a number of issues:

- The resultant application is tied to the distribution framework in such a way that it is generally impossible to replace one distribution implementation with another without a significant refactoring effort.
- The resultant application's business logic is tangled with the distribution concern making reuse of the business logic in other domains problematic, if not impossible.
- Distribution frameworks impose a large code overhead due to the requirements distributed systems impose, such as the need to catch distribution specific exceptions, locating and binding to distributed objects, locating another server in the event the current server becomes unavailable and adhering to programming conventions dictated by the framework, such as implementing framework specific interfaces.

In addition, the scattering and tangling of distribution frameworks throughout an application violates the principle of separation of concerns, a guiding principle of software engineering that allows one to identify, encapsulate, and manipulate only those parts of software that are relevant to a particular goal or purpose [79]. Concerns that are scattered and tangled throughout an application in this way are referred to as *crosscutting concerns* [31].

There are essentially two extremes, in terms of distribution awareness, that one could take in the development of distributed applications. The first, pioneered by the use of the Remote Procedure Call (RPC) paradigm, attempts to make the network transparent to the programmer by masking the difference between local and remote procedure calls. Many distributed systems, such as the Open Network Computing (ONC) system [98], have adopted this philosophy.

The second extreme approach, pioneered by the developers of Java's RMI, argues that applications need to be aware of the distribution concern because there are fundamental differences between the interactions of distributed objects and the interactions of non-distributed objects, such as latency, different calling semantics, and partial failures [118]. Consequently Java's RMI framework, and associated technologies that depend upon it, require that the developer be aware of remote objects and remote errors that may occur while interacting with remote objects. This approach is highly intrusive as the developer is required to implement specific interfaces, catch remote exceptions, and, in some cases, inherit from the distribution framework.

We believe that both of these methods are unsatisfactory. On the one hand, the attempt to make the network transparent results in brittle applications and on the other, the distribution framework is tangled with the application, thereby violating the concept of separation of concerns, making reuse of the application's components difficult and the use of a different distribution framework without significant refactoring almost impossible. Both of these extremes, and variations in-between, result in applications that are polluted with the distribution concern. The resultant applications, and associated components, are therefore difficult to reuse in other domains, difficult to extend and difficult to maintain.

Aspect-oriented Programming and the Distribution Concern

Aspect-Oriented Programming (AOP) [59], a fairly recent innovation in software development, attempts to isolate and modularise crosscutting concerns, termed *aspects*, by composing them into modules and applying the aspects to existing code. By doing so, the code only performs its intended function and is not 'polluted' with the crosscutting concern. The additional modularisation capability introduced by aspects provides the ability to apply crosscutting concerns in a non-invasive way resulting in applications that are easier to maintain, extend and reuse.

Distribution is considered a crosscutting concern and seminal work in AOP concentrated on modularising the distribution concern [66]. Since then, several attempts have been made to apply the distribution concern to existing code using AOP techniques. These attempts have generally concentrated on applying aspects to existing code that has not been written with distribution in mind. This attempt at distribution transparency has significant issues, similar to those identified by Waldo et al. [118], because distributed method calls do not behave in the same way as local method calls.

We have also found during our research that applications that have not been written with distribution in mind can, once distribution has been applied, have undesirable side effects. For example, a class that starts threads in its constructor will, once methods in the class are made distributed, start these threads in both the client and server because the, now distributed, object must be instantiated on both the client and the server. In addition, if methods are not at the correct level of granularity, for example too coarse or too fine grained, then distribution cannot be applied efficiently or effectively or at all. For these reasons, we believe distribution transparency is neither desirable nor achievable in all circumstances.

Autonomic Computing

The vision of autonomic computing [52, 56] is to reduce the configuration, operational and maintenance costs of distributed systems by enabling systems to self-manage, self-heal and self-optimise [121].

However, a key challenge limiting the use of autonomic features in applications is the lack of tools and frameworks that can alleviate the complexities stemming from the use of manual development methods [56].

This is evident in current distributed systems development techniques, which require the manual use of tools and frameworks and therefore cannot meet the challenges posed by the autonomic computing vision. Consequently, alternative methods of distributed systems development are needed to meet these challenges.

To meet the autonomic computing vision of self-managing, self-healing and self-optimising systems requires a system to be able to dynamically adapt to its environment and the majority of adaptions that are used in autonomic systems, such as caching, security, persistence, distribution etc., tend to be crosscutting in nature [44, 69].

Aspect-oriented programming, by allowing crosscutting concerns to be modularised and added to existing code, has long been realised as a viable method for developing adaptive autonomic systems [69].

1.1   Research Goal

The primary goal of our research is to provide a contribution to the development of autonomic systems by exploring an alternative approach to the development of distributed applications which allows:

- An application, written with distribution in mind, to be made distributed using any one of a number of distribution frameworks interchangeably.
- Distributed versions of an application to participate in distribution recovery scenarios without the underlying application code having to be aware of recovery.
- The same application to be used either distributed or non-distributed, thereby improving software reuse and simplifying testing.

1.2   Overview of Approach

For this research we have chosen to use the Java programming language as most types of distributed systems technology are available for Java and primary research into aspect-oriented systems either use Java as the underlying programming language or extend it. However, we believe the concepts defined in this research are applicable to other environments.

To achieve our goals of applying the distribution concern to existing Java code, while allowing full participation in recovery scenarios without the underlying code being aware of either the distribution protocol or the recovery scenario, we use the following approach:

- We ensure that new applications are written with distribution in mind and existing applications are refactored for distribution; that is that methods that will become distributed are exposed at the correct level of granularity, that threading and object consistency are catered to, and that the method's return value and parameters implement the `java.io.Serializable` interface, if applicable.
- We introduce the concept of a Distribution Definition Language, a high-level *domain-specific aspect language*, which describes the classes and methods of an existing application that are to be made remote, the distributed system to use to make them remote and the recovery mechanism to use in the event of a remote error.
- We introduce a software tool in the form of the RemoteJ compiler/generator that uses information contained in the Distribution Definition Language to generate the distributed system specific code and apply it to the application using bytecode manipulation and generation techniques.

1.3   Limitations

There are a number of limitations to our approach, described in detail in Section 4.5 and Section 5.7, which may be summarised as:

Concurrency. As our approach is to ensure that applications are written with distribution in mind and current Java distribution protocols do not support distributed thread co-ordination, we do not specifically address concurrency. We discuss this in detail in Section 4.5.3.

Object passing. Some protocols, such as RMI, pass parameters and return values by value or by reference. In the case of RMI, if the object is a remote object (implements the `java.rmi.Remote` interface), a reference to the object is passed in a remote call, otherwise a copy of the object is passed. As pass-by-value is supported by all protocols we have implemented, we currently do not support pass-by-reference. Protocol agnostic pass-by-reference support is an area for future research.

Callbacks. We do not currently provide support for callbacks where a server calls back into a client or is a client to another server. This limits the class of applications that our approach may be applied to and is an area for further research.

1.4   Hypothesis Statement

We contend that the distribution and recovery concerns can be completely and effectively modularised by defining them in a high-level domain-specific aspect language which can be applied to existing applications using a compiler/generator tool.

We evaluate the above approach and show that a Distribution Definition Language contributes to autonomic computing by simplifying the development of distributed applications while allowing for greater reuse of application components.

1.5   Contribution

The contributions of this research include the following:

1. The concept of a Distribution Definition Language used to define classes and associated methods to be made distributed, the distributed system to use to make them distributed, and the recovery mechanism to use in the event of an error.
2. A simplified approach to the development of distributed systems that allows an existing application to be distributed, thereby improving software reusability and simplifying testability of distributed applications, as applications may be functionally tested before having the distribution and recovery concerns applied.
3. The ability to apply one of a number of protocols to the same code base thereby generalising the distribution concern.
4. The ability to apply distribution awareness to applications in such a way that the application is oblivious to the distribution implementation and recovery mechanism, yet is able to fully participate in both.

In addition, these contributions, by alleviating some of the complexity involved in distributed systems development and by allowing autonomic features, such as recovery, to be transparently added to existing applications, provides a contribution to autonomic computing.

1.6   Publications Overview

This book is an extension of the author's Ph.D. thesis and the Distribution Definition Language was first described in a paper presented at the Domain-Specific

Aspect Language (DSAL) workshop at the international Aspect-Oriented Software Development (AOSD) conference. References to these papers are:

- Soule, P., T. Carnduff, and S. Lewis, A Distribution Definition Language for the Automated Distribution of Java Objects, in *Proceedings of the 2nd workshop on Domain Specific Aspect Languages, AOSD '07*, Vancouver, British Columbia, Canada. ACM Press, 2007
- Soule, P., A Domain-Specific Aspect Language Approach to Distributed Systems Development, Ph.D. thesis, University of Glamorgan, Pontypridd Wales, United Kingdom, 2008

The workshop paper may be downloaded from the ACM library at the following URL:

http://portal.acm.org.

The thesis may be obtained directly from the institution concerned or the British Library Electronic Thesis Online Service at the following URL:

http://ethos.bl.uk.

1.7   Book Structure

This book is structured as follows. In Chapter 2 we discuss issues surrounding distributed systems development and the background and motivation for our work. Chapter 3 gives a broad overview of aspect-oriented programming and its use in distributed systems development. Chapter 4 describes the Distribution Definition Language, its features, and motivation. In Chapter 5 we describe the RemoteJ compiler/generator implementation and its features. In Chapter 6 we evaluate our implementation. Finally, in Chapter 7 we provide a summary and present our conclusions.

Autonomics Development: A Domain-Specific Aspect Language Approach, 7–39
Book Series: Autonomic Systems
© 2010 Springer Basel AG

2 Distributed Systems Development

2.1 Introduction

Computer systems used to be expensive standalone self-contained entities, each with its own disk storage, line printers, terminals and other peripherals. The introduction of the minicomputer made computers cheaper and more widespread, which led to the requirement to share information between them. This requirement led to the development of early computer networks, such as the Unix-to-Unix copy program (UUCP) in 1976 and its subsequent release in AT&T Version 7 Unix in the same year.

The development of Berknet by Eric Schmidt in 1978 at the University of California, Berkeley and its subsequent distribution in Version 7 Unix for the PDP-11 minicomputer allowed users to send and receive email, transfer files and print remotely [88]. In 1980, Bolt, Beranek, and Newman were contracted by the American Department of Defense to implement the TCP/IP protocol for BSD UNIX. The release of 4.2BSD in August 1983 with its implementation of TCP/IP and the BSD sockets programming model, coupled with the growth of local area networks based mainly on Ethernet, allowed computers to connect to the ARPANET, the predecessor to the Internet, which led to the enormous growth of networked systems in the early 1980s [96].

The introduction of the personal computer and its subsequent ability to connect to TCP/IP networks using the Winsock API, based on BSD sockets, led to a huge increase in the number of networked machines and distributed systems began to become mainstream. Automated teller machines, airline reservation systems, file sharing, file transfer, centralised database access, email and various other distributed systems were introduced.

The subsequent invention of the web browser and HTTP protocol led to the World Wide Web and the enormous explosion in the number of distributed systems that we see today. With the continued increase in processing power and fall in component prices, computing is promising to become even more widespread and we may well see the vision of ubiquitous computing [120] being met in the future. Yet, while distributed systems have become mainstream, distributed systems development remains difficult and little advancement has been made since the initial concepts were developed decades ago.

This chapter develops the lineage towards the domain-specific aspect language (DSAL) approach to distributed systems development by examining previous approaches, and issues surrounding those approaches.

We begin by discussing the low-level Application Programming Interface (API) approach as exemplified by BSD sockets. We then discuss the RPC approach for both procedural languages, in the form of ONC RPC, and object-oriented systems in the form of CORBA and Java RMI and compare the network awareness and network transparent models.

We then discuss the high-level API approach as exemplified by JMS and discuss the effects and implications the different approaches have on ease of development, software reusability and maintainability.

Throughout this chapter we use the example of a simple distributed service that returns the current date.

2.2   Sockets-Based Programming

Sockets are a low-level generalised programming interface for networking and interprocess communication first provided in the BSD4.2 operating system[1]. Most, if not all, UNIX systems provide the socket API and various operating systems, such as Windows with its Winsock API, provide similar functionality.

Sockets are a low-level networking API modelled on the UNIX systems calls related to file I/O semantics. While there is some similarity between file and network I/O operations, network I/O has other considerations, which make the fit less than perfect. Stevens [96] identifies the following considerations for network I/O:

- The client server relationship is not symmetrical. The application needs to know which role (client or server) it is to assume.
- Network connections can be connectionless or connection-oriented. Connectionless operations do not map neatly to file operations because there is no concept of opening a connection as every network I/O operation could be to a different host.
- Names are more important in distributed systems, for example to verify security, than they are for file operations. Therefore, passing a file descriptor to a process without knowing the original name, while being acceptable for a file I/O operation, may not be acceptable for a network I/O operation.
- Additional parameters, for example the protocol and its details, are required for network operations.
- While the UNIX I/O system is stream-oriented, many network protocols are message-oriented and therefore rely on message boundaries.

---

[1]Strictly speaking, BSD sockets were initially provided in the 4.1cBSD release and subsequently refined into their current form in 4.2BSD.

- Network interfaces support multiple protocols, each with differing addressing requirements so that, for example, a 32-bit identifier is not sufficient for holding network addresses for all protocols. Network interfaces therefore need to be generalised.

Sockets provide a low-level interface to network protocols. For anything other than simple message exchanges, protocols are developed to exchange messages in specific formats. Due to the stream-oriented nature of the UNIX I/O system, this is a particularly onerous task as the programmer is required to implement packet assembly and disassembly, which differs depending on the protocol being implemented. In addition, error handling and recovery is left entirely up to the programmer, making socket development difficult and error prone.

This section provides an overview and evaluation of the BSD socket interface and illustrates its usage through a simple application.

2.2.1   BSD Socket Interface

As previously mentioned, there are a number of similarities between file and network I/O operations. The BSD socket interface attempts to provide as much similarity as possible while allowing additional network-based operations. Table 2.1 provides an overview of the differences and similarities between the socket and file operations.

Figure 2.1 provides an overview of the steps required for both client and server to initiate a transfer for a connection-oriented transfer. This interaction can be summarised as:

Server interaction. Firstly, the server obtains a socket via the socket() call and then bind() is called, which assigns a name to the socket. Next listen() is called to indicate that the application is willing to accept connection requests. As well as the socket, the listen() call also accepts a backlog parameter, which stipulates the number of connection requests that can be queued by the system while it waits for the accept() call to be executed. If a connection attempt arrives and the queue is full, the connection is refused. Finally accept() is called, which suspends the application until a connection request arrives from the client.

Client interaction. A socket is obtained via the socket() call and then connect() is called with a parameter stipulating the socket and the address of the server. The address is passed in the sockaddr structure and contains the local address, the remote address, and the protocol to use. Once a connection has been established, messages can be exchanged between the two systems. For both of the above, the close() call can be used to close the connection and the shutdown() call can be used to close part of the connection, either reads or writes.

The socket API also provides the select() function, which is used to provide I/O multiplexing by allowing the programmer to examine a set of file descriptors

TABLE 2.1. Comparison of file and socket calls.

Operation	Files	Sockets	
Open	open()	Client	socket() bind() connect()
		Server	socket() bind() listen() accept()
Close	close()	close() shutdown()	
Read	read()	read() recv() recvfrom()	
Write	write()	write() send() sendto()	
Seek	lseek()		
Poll	select()	select()	
Create	creat()		

to see if they are ready for I/O or if certain events have occurred. UNIX systems also provide asynchronous I/O which is used in conjunction with select() thereby allowing a single process to efficiently handle a large number of open files or sockets simultaneously.

2.2.2   Socket Example

Our simple example provides the current system date to a client on demand and prints it to the console. The protocol we use between client and server is based on the exchange of C style strings between client and server. While this may sound simple, it is not, due to fundamental differences between file I/O and network I/O even though both share the same interface.

Using sockets, a read or write call may input or output fewer bytes than requested due to underlying kernel buffer limits. However, a read operation from a file is guaranteed to return the number of bytes requested providing that the number requested is less than or equal to that remaining before end-of-file. In the event a read or write call returns fewer bytes than expected, the call must be invoked again to receive or send the remaining bytes [96]. This can significantly complicate socket development, particularly if the protocol developed contains many different packet types of different sizes and advanced features such as slidingwindows and

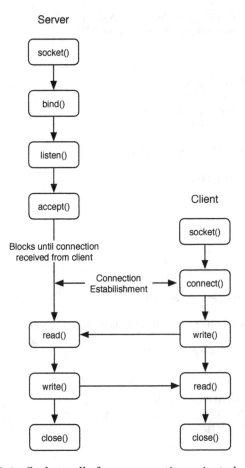

FIGURE 2.1. Socket calls for a connection-oriented protocol.

piggybacking [107] are used. To overcome this, we provide a set of utility routines to read the remaining bytes, in the case of a read call, or output the remaining bytes, in the case of a write call.

```
int readline(int socket, char *buffer, int len);
int writeline(int socket, char * buffer, int bytes);
```

Our server implementation is as follows:

```
extern int writeline(int socket, char * buffer, int bytes);

int main(int argc, char ** argv) {

    int sock;
    struct sockaddr_in server;
```

```
if ((sock = socket(AF_INET, SOCK_STREAM, 0)) < 0) {
    fprintf(stderr, "cannot open stream socket\n");
    exit(1);
}

memset(&server, 0, sizeof(server));
server.sin_family = AF_INET;
server.sin_addr.s_addr = htonl(INADDR_ANY);
server.sin_port = htons(5000);

if (bind(sock, (struct sockaddr *) &server,
            sizeof(server)) < 0) {
    fprintf(stderr, "bind failed\n");
    exit(1);
}

listen(sock, 10);

for(;;) {
    struct sockaddr_in client;
    int fd;
    unsigned int client_len = sizeof(client);

    fd = accept(sock, (struct sockaddr *) &client, &client_len);
    if (fd < 0) {
        fprintf(stderr, "accept failed");
        exit(1);
    }

    time_t now = time(NULL);
    char *s = ctime(&now);
    writeline(fd, s, strlen(s));

    close(fd);
}
}
```

The client implementation is as follows:

```
extern int readline(int socket, char * buffer, int bytes);

int main(int argc, char ** argv) { int sock; struct sockaddr_in
    server;

    memset(&server, 0, sizeof(server));
    server.sin_family = AF_INET;
    server.sin_addr.s_addr = inet_addr("127.0.0.1");
    server.sin_port = htons(5000);

    if ((sock = socket(AF_INET, SOCK_STREAM, 0)) < 0) {
        fprintf(stderr, "cannot open stream socket\n");
        exit(1);
    }
```

```
if (connect(sock, (struct sockaddr *) &server,
            sizeof(server)) < 0) {
    fprintf(stderr, "connect failed\n");
    exit(1);
}

char buf [512];

readline(sock, buf, sizeof(buf));
printf("The time on the server is: %s", buf);

close(sock);
exit(0);
}
```

In both the client and the server examples above, the code that is used to either obtain the date or receive it is shaded in grey, while the other code implements the distribution concern.

2.2.3   Summary

Socket-based programming is highly complex and error prone. Developers need to implement message-based protocols on top of the socket interface with the resultant complexity directly proportional to the protocol requirements.

As illustrated in our simple example, socket-based programming is highly intrusive, even for simple applications. Programmers need to adhere to the socket API throughout the application and ensure that reads from sockets and writes to sockets return the number of bytes requested or the number of bytes required to be written respectively.

The most common protocols used in socket programming are TCP/IP and UDP/IP. UDP is a datagram protocol, which does not provide guaranteed message delivery or duplicate elimination. Although TCP/IP provides these features it does not guarantee message delivery in all circumstances [23, 115]. If guaranteed message delivery is a protocol requirement, it will need to be provided by the protocol developer. Protocol reliability is discussed in detail in Section 2.3.4.

Recovery is left up to the programmer to implement at a very low level and any significant recovery routines, for example connecting to another server in the event the current server becomes unavailable, will have to be implemented wherever a remote call is made, thereby further complicating development.

2.3   Remote Procedure Calls

In order to provide an environment with the simplicity of the then dominant procedural programming paradigm, Birrell and Nelson [15] suggested the use of remote procedure calls (RPC). The idea of RPCs is based on the observation that procedure calls are a well-known and well-understood mechanism for transfer of control and data within a program running on a single system and that this mechanism can be extended to be used across a communications network [15]. By extending procedure calls to a distributed environment, interprocess communication is then given the syntax and semantics of a well-accepted strongly typed language abstraction [90].

According to Soares [90], the RPC mechanism has the following advantages:

- The communication mechanism has clean, general, and comprehensible semantics.
- A programmer is able to design a distributed application using the same abstraction as well-engineered software in a non-distributed application.
- It provides *information hiding* as information can be hidden within design components.
- The distribution of the application is transparent to the application user and all communication details are hidden.

When a remote procedure call is invoked, the calling environment is suspended, the procedure parameters are passed across the network to the callee, and the procedure is executed on the remote machine. When the procedure finishes, the results are passed back to the calling environment, where execution resumes as if returning from a local procedure call [15].

RPCs can be either asynchronous or synchronous. Asynchronous RPC calls do not block the caller and the replies can be received as and when they are needed, thus allowing the caller execution to proceed in parallel with the callee execution [4]. With synchronous RPCs, on the other hand, the caller is blocked until the callee has finished execution.

This section provides an overview of the remote procedure call paradigm and an implementation of a simple application using the ONC RPC system. We describe the features and facilities of RPC systems along with their shortcomings and compare it to BSD socket-based distributed systems.

2.3.1   Stubs and Skeletons

Remote procedure calls achieve a high-level of abstraction by using a system based on proxies [41]. Proxies are used on the caller side to convert local procedure calls into remote procedure calls and are used on the callee side to convert remote procedure calls to local procedure calls. The caller proxy is known as a *stub* and the callee proxy is known as a *skeleton* [116]. The interaction[2] between the components in an RPC system is depicted in the diagram in Figure 2.2.

When a remote procedure call is invoked, the stub (compiled into the caller code) translates the arguments into a data representation, a process called marshalling, and transmits the data to the callee via the RPCRuntime system. On receipt of the packets, the RPCRuntime in the callee machine passes them to the skeleton (compiled into the callee code). The skeleton unpacks them into the

---

[2]This example adapted from Birrell and Nelson [15].

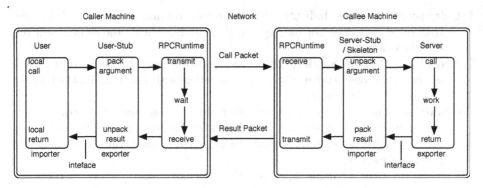

FIGURE 2.2. RPC components and their interactions.

appropriate data types for the machine, a process known as unmarshalling, and makes a normal local procedure call to the server process. The return value from the local procedure call is then marshalled by the skeleton and returned to the calling code [15, 116].

2.3.2 Interface Definition Language

Remote procedure calls generally make no assumptions about the architecture of the remote system or the programming language remote procedures have been written in. Key to supporting communication between these systems of unknown architectures written in unknown programming languages is the notion of an Interface Definition Language (IDL), a machine-neutral language used to describe the remote procedures, their parameters, and the call semantics (described in Section 2.3.4) in a machine neutral way. The IDL is read by an application, which generates the stubs and skeletons of the application.

The Network Interface Definition Language (NIDL) defined as part of the Network Computing Architecture (NCA) [26] provides the following data types:

Integers: Both signed and unsigned integers in one, two, four, and eight byte sizes.
Floating point: Single (four byte) and double (eight byte) precision floating point.
Scalar types: Other scalars including signed and unsigned characters, booleans, and enumerations.
Type constructors: Structures, discriminated unions, pointers, and arrays. Pointers to pointers or records containing pointers are not permitted.

Various attributes can be associated with remote procedures so that the RPC compiler can generate stubs and skeletons that are either more efficient or provide a particular feature. For example, the Distributed Computing Environment (DCE) [109] provides the following attributes:

The idempotent attribute: Indicates that the operation may safely be called more than once as it does not modify any state and/or yields the same result on each invocation.

The broadcast attribute: Specifies that the operation may be sent to multiple servers, effectively concurrently. An operation with the broadcast attribute is implicitly an idempotent operation.

The maybe attribute: Specifies that the operation's caller must not require and must not receive a response or fault indication. An operation with the maybe attribute must not contain any output parameters and is implicitly an idempotent operation.

The reflect_deletions attribute: Specifies that memory occupied by targets of pointers on the client will be released when the corresponding targets of pointers on the server are released. This is true only for targets that are components of in-parameters of the operation.

Having a machine-neutral IDL allows multiple languages to use the RPC system as the IDL compilers can generate the stubs and skeletons for each implementation language. This also has the advantage of allowing a remote procedure developed in one language to communicate with a remote procedure developed in another language.

While this greatly simplifies the development of distributed applications, the language-neutral nature limits the kinds of data that can be exchanged between processes to the basic data types that can be represented in all the target languages [116].

While IDLs remove the complexity of network data representation from the programmer, the programmer must still control the lifecycle management of the data sent that typically require either complex conventions or reference counting. These procedures are prone to programmer error that can lead to memory leaks or referential integrity loss [116].

2.3.3 Data Representation

Due to the heterogeneous nature of computer networks, data transmitted between machines require a data representation protocol, which defines the way data is represented so that machines that store data in different internal formats are able to communicate [26].

There are a number of data representation standards including Sun's XDR standard [97] and DCE's NDR [109].

2.3.4 Calls Semantics

Due to their distributed nature, remote procedure calls can fail. According to Soares [90], there are three causes of RPC failure:

Network failure: The network is unavailable and the caller and callee cannot send or receive data.

Caller site failure: The caller process fails or the host running the caller process fails.

Callee site failure: The callee process fails or the host running the callee process fails. In this case, the caller may be indefinitely suspended awaiting a response from the callee.

Most RPC systems, such as DCE RPC [109], attempt to hide their distributed nature from the programmer so that, to the programmer, the RPC system is transparent. The RPC system, and not the application code, is therefore responsible for ensuring a message reaches its intended destination and a response is received.

If, however, no response is received within a specific timeout period, one of four different conditions may have occurred [90]:

1. The callee did not receive the request.
2. The callee received the request and acted upon it but the caller did not receive the response.
3. The callee failed during the execution of the call and either resumed execution of the call upon restarting or did not.
4. The callee was still busy executing the call when the caller timed out.

According to Soares [90], a major design decision for an RPC mechanism is the choice of call semantics in the presence of failures. Spector [95] defines four different call semantics:

Maybe: The callee does not return a response to the caller and the caller receives no indication of success or failure.

At least once: The remote procedure is executed at least once.

Only once type 1: This is commonly referred to as at most once [108]. The remote procedure is executed at most once.

Only once type 2: This is commonly referred to as exactly once [108]. The call has been executed once only.

Although exactly once call semantics are generally considered to only be possible using asynchronous procedure calls [95], a number of attempts have been made to provide exactly once semantics for synchronous procedure calls.

Heindel and Kasten [48] have implemented reliable synchronous RPC calls for DCE by imposing a middleware layer between the caller and callee. This middleware layer, however, uses asynchronous messaging to achieve this reliability and therefore can be considered asynchronous in implementation.

The Encina transaction monitor attempts to implement reliable synchronous messaging using an extension of DCE's RPC, called TRPC – transactional RPC [89]. This approach is, in many ways, similar to the asynchronous approach as transactions are written to a log file before being committed. Other approaches, such as replicated procedure calls, have been implemented [22]. Unfortunately this results in a high overhead per operation (O) as the number of messages (M) required to complete a request (N) is ($O(M \times N)$) [90].

Synchronous RPC systems can generally be considered suitable[3] only for applications that can be modelled as idempotent, that is they can safely execute the same procedure more than once without any adverse effects. Probably the best known example is Sun's Network File System (NFS) [99].

2.3.5   Binding

Binding refers to the process used to identity and address remote procedures. Bindings are either performed statically, during compilation, or dynamically, at runtime. Callees advertise their bindings, or location, in a naming service so that callers are able to find them, based on appropriate search criteria [109].

In order to find the callee the caller needs to provide, depending on the implementation, either the specific server process of the callee, the name of the machine where the callee is located, or just the name of the procedure to be called [90].

Attributes may be associated with bindings, for example a version number, so that the caller may choose which specific instance to bind to. Once bound, the remote procedure may be called.

2.3.6   Open Network Computing (ONC) Example

The following is an overview of the development of our simple distributed application using Sun's Open Network Computing (ONC) system [98], a widely deployed RPC implementation which was originally developed for Sun's NFS.

2.3.6.1   ONC IDL

The IDL used by ONC describes remote procedures, their arguments and return values, associated version numbers and a unique program number identifier. To implement our simple example, we firstly declare the remote procedure in ONC IDL as follows:

```
program GETDATE_PROG {
  version DETDATE_VERS {
    string GETDATE(void) = 1;
  } = 1;
} = 22855;
```

The above IDL fragment defines version .1 of a remote procedure called GET-DATE, which has the parameter type void and returns the current date as a string.

---

[3]Although reliable synchronous RPC systems do exist, they either require the programmer to handle timeouts, retransmissions, and the receipt and sending of messages (removing much of the advantage of using an RPC system) or rely on other mechanisms, such as replication, which significantly increase complexity and have adverse effects on performance.

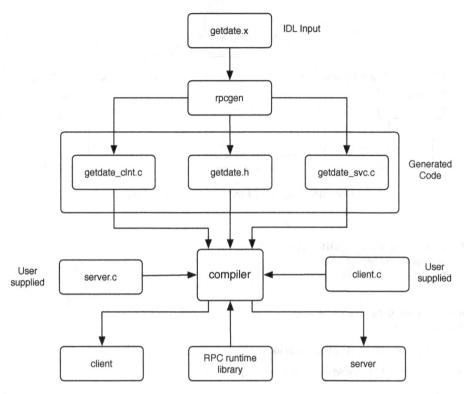

FIGURE 2.3. Sun ONC RPC generator.

The unique program number for our implementation is 22855. The **rpcgen** program is then run against the IDL file, which generates a header file **getdate.h**, and two skeleton files, **getdate_clnt.c** and **getdate_svc.c** for the client and server implementations respectively as illustrated in Figure 2.3.

The generated files contain the marshalling and unmarshalling, binding, data representation (XDR), and framework integration code required to implement the ONC protocol.

2.3.6.2 ONC Example Implementation

The files generated by the **rpcgen** application are required to be linked with user-supplied files for the client and server implementation. For our example, the relevant portion of our client implementation is as follows:

```
if ((cl = clnt_create(server, GETDATE_PROG,
        GETDATE_VERS, "udp")) == NULL) {
    clnt_pcreateerror(server);
    exit(1);
}
```

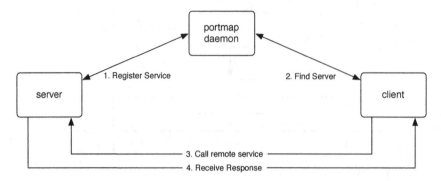

FIGURE 2.4. Sun ONC runtime binding.

```
if ((message = getdate_1(NULL, cl)) == NULL) {
    clnt_perror(cl, server);
    exit(1);
}

printf("Server Date: %s\n", *message);
clnt_destroy(cl);
```

and our server implementation:

```
char ** getdate_1_svc(void *v, struct svc_req *svc) {

    time_t now = time(NULL);
    static char *date;
    date = ctime(&now);

    return (&date);
}
```

Note that both the client and server implementation code is required to adhere to the ONC specific framework and programming conventions. For example, in the server implementation, the value that is returned to the client is required to be **static** and the function signature is required to use the framework specific structure **svc_req** and to have the program's version number appended. For the client implementation, the client is required to call the ONC framework directly, as illustrated by the **clnt_create** function call in our example. However, for the server code no protocol specific code is required.

ONC servers advertise their presence in the portmap service so that clients may find them. At runtime clients bind to the portmap server, which provides the address of the server to clients as illustrated in Figure 2.4. Clients then connect directly to the server.

2.3.7   Summary

This section has provided an overview of the remote procedure call paradigm and an implementation of our simple example using the ONC RPC system. Various aspects of RPC systems have been discussed including the IDL, data representation and call semantics.

As illustrated in our example, RPC systems are highly intrusive as programmers are required to describe their remote procedures in an IDL, to implement methods generated by the IDL program generator, to use the RPC framework directly in the implementation code, and to adhere to framework specific conventions. However, compared to BSD socket-based systems, RPC systems are significantly easier to implement, understand, and subsequently maintain.

Most RPC systems attempt to provide programmer transparency so that calling a remote procedure is as simple as calling a local procedure. Indeed, this transparency is often seen as a great benefit of the RPC paradigm as Soares [90] states:

> "The ideal RPC mechanism is the one that provides the application user with the same syntax and semantics for all procedure calls independently of being a local call or a remote one"

This notion of transparency, however, leads to an unfortunate situation when errors occur, as recovery is left to the RPC system to handle, not the programmer. Unfortunately, in many situations, the RPC system simply cannot recover, resulting in the application hanging while the RPC runtime attempts to reconnect to the server. Synchronous RPC systems are therefore suitable only for applications that can be modelled as idempotent, such as the NFS system. Perhaps the biggest weakness with RPC systems, however, is that their language-neutral nature limits the data types that can travel between processes to the basic static data types that can be supported by each language [116].

2.4   CORBA

One of the primary issues with early RPC systems is that they did not have an object-oriented model and client applications need to know not only how to access a server but also the location of the server. In addition, client code has to change whenever the client wants to use new services [27].

The Common Object Request Broker Architecture (CORBA) is designed as a *middleware* to enable distributed objects to communicate with one another via an Object Request Broker (ORB). In the CORBA model, clients communicate to a server via an ORB as illustrated in Figure 2.5.

Communicating via an ORB removes the necessity for a client to know the whereabouts of a server as clients send requests to the ORB requesting that certain

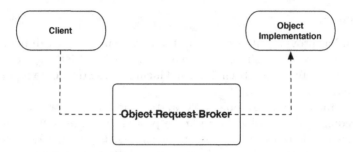

FIGURE 2.5. A request being sent via the ORB.

services be performed. The ORB then passes those requests on to a server, which acts upon it, and passes the result back to the client via the ORB.

The ORB is responsible for the mechanisms required to find the object implementation for the request, to prepare the object implementation to receive the request, and to communicate the data making up the request. The interface the client sees is completely independent of where the object is located, what programming language it is implemented in, or any other aspect that is not reflected in the object's interface [77].

Clients, therefore, only know the location of the ORB and the ORB knows the implementation details and locations of the servers. Clients and servers communicate only via component interfaces and any changes in object implementation or location are insulated from the client [27, 75, 77].

CORBA is a heterogeneous system that can be run on many different platforms and CORBA applications may be written in many different languages. For this reason CORBA uses an IDL, similar to RPC type systems. The main construct in the CORBA IDL is the *interface* which defines the various operations that may be called by clients. Once written, the IDL is run through a compiler to generate code for the particular implementation language [7]. By using a language and machine independent IDL, clients and servers may be written in different languages and may be run on different operating systems so that it is possible for, say, a client writing in the C language running under the UNIX operating system to communicate to a server writing in Java running under the Windows operating system.

One of the more interesting aspects of CORBA is that it uses an object-oriented architecture in that it adds a notion of inheritance. In CORBA IDL an interface may inherit from another interface as shown in Figure 2.6.

In addition, CORBA IDL supports *multiple inheritance* where an interface may inherit from several different interfaces. There are, however, a number of limitations to the multiple inheritance feature of the CORBA IDL [7]:

- An IDL interface cannot redefine an operation or attribute in a derived interface.
- It is illegal for an interface to inherit from two interfaces that have a common operation or attribute name.

```
interface Vehicle {
};

interface Car : Vehicle {
};
```

FIGURE 2.6. An example of the CORBA IDL's support for inheritance.

Servers that implement derived interfaces, however, are considered an implementation of the basic interface, which gives a notion of polymorphism as the server is treated as though it were of both the base type and the derived type within the CORBA architecture [122].

2.4.1   CORBA Event Service

Standard CORBA requests are synchronous in nature. A request is sent from a client to a server via the ORB and the client suspends awaiting a response from the server. In this scenario, both client and server must be available.

The CORBA event service [76] decouples communication between clients and servers using either the *push model* or the *pull model*.

The push model allows the supplier of events to initiate the transfer of event data to consumers, while the pull model reverses this by allowing the event consumer to request event data from the producer.

The CORBA event architecture uses an *event channel*, an intervening object that allows producers and consumers to communicate asynchronously. This architecture is illustrated in Figure 2.7.

2.4.2   CORBA Example IDL

In order to implement our simple date application, we are firstly required to define the CORBA interface in an IDL file[4]. Figure 2.8 illustrates the IDL implementation for our simple example.

Our IDL defines a simple interface with two operations, `getDate()`, our method to return the server's date and `shutdown()`, a method used to shut down the ORB.

Once we have defined the IDL we run the IDL through the `idlj` compiler to generate CORBA helper files that are necessary to implement the client and server code. Once run, the `idlj` compiler generates the following files:

---

[4]This example is derived from [101].

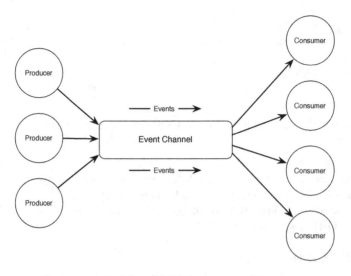

FIGURE 2.7. The CORBA event architecture.

```
module DateApp {
  interface Date {
    string getDate();
    oneway void shutdown();
  };
};
```

FIGURE 2.8. The IDL for our simple CORBA implementation

- `DatePOA.java`. An abstract class that provides basic CORBA functionality for the server. It extends `org.omg.PortableServer.Servant`, and implements the `InvokeHandler` interface and the `DateOperations` interface. The server class, `DateServant`, extends `DatePOA`.
- `_DateStub.java`. The client stub which is used to provide CORBA functionality for the client. It extends `org.omg.CORBA.portable.ObjectImpl` and implements the `Date` interface.
- `Date.java`. This is an interface that contains the Java version of the IDL interface and extends `org.omg.CORBA.Object`, providing standard CORBA object functionality, and the `DateOperations` interface and `org.omg.CORBA.portable.IDLEntity` class.
- `DateHelper.java`. This class provides auxiliary functionality, such as the `narrow()` method used to cast CORBA object references to their proper types.

- `DateHolder.java`. This class holds a public instance member of type `Date` and is used for all operations that have an `inout` IDL declaration.
- `Operations.java`. This interface contains the methods `getDate()` and `shutdown()` and is shared by both the stubs and skeletons.

2.4.3   CORBA Example Implementation

Our server implementation is illustrated in Figure 2.9 and our client implementation in Figure 2.10. As can be seen by these examples, Java's CORBA framework is highly intrusive in nature, requiring the developer to implement the framework's code alongside the applications leading to a tight coupling between the application and the distribution framework.

To run the CORBA example, the ORB needs to be started and the server bound to the ORB. Once bound, the client application connects to the ORB and requests the service it is interested in by name. The ORB contacts the server, which runs the request and sends the result back to the ORB. The ORB then returns the result back to the requesting client.

2.4.4   Summary

CORBA has similar issues to RPC type systems in that the range of values that can be passed between systems, either as arguments or return values, is limited to those that can be represented in all of the implementation languages supported. In addition, as with all IDLs, programmers have an additional language to learn and an additional artefact to deal with. A limitation with the object-oriented nature of CORBA is that objects are passed by *reference* not by *value*. There is also no way to extend the range of permissible values transmitted on the fly and still ensure that the value will be correctly interpreted upon receipt [122].

As can be seen in our simple CORBA example, Java's CORBA framework imposes a large overhead as well as a great deal of complexity. As is common with all frameworks, the CORBA framework is highly intrusive in nature, as illustrated by the shaded areas in Figures 2.9 and 2.10, and results in CORBA specific code tangled with the application's code making reuse of the application code extremely difficult.

2.5   Java Remote Method Invocation (RMI)

Object-oriented systems are currently the dominant programming paradigm and a number of distributed systems exist for object-oriented languages and systems. Many of these systems use the RPC mechanism even though procedure calls, as such, no longer exist in the object-oriented paradigm. Consequently many of these systems do not provide object-oriented features, such as polymorphism, because the RPC type paradigm only allows for the *static* representation of data [116].

```
import DateApp.*;
import org.omg.CosNaming.*;
import org.omg.CORBA.*;
import org.omg.PortableServer.*;
import org.omg.PortableServer.POA;

class HelloImpl extends DatePOA {
    private ORB orb;

    public void setORB(ORB orb_val) {
        orb = orb_val;
    }

    public String getDate() {
        return new java.util.Date().toString();
    }

    public void shutdown() {
        orb.shutdown(false);
    }
}

public class DateServer {

    public static void main(String args[]) {
        try {
            ORB orb = ORB.init(args, null);
            POA rootpoa =
                    POAHelper.narrow(orb.resolve_initial_references("RootPOA"));
            rootpoa.the_POAManager().activate();
            HelloImpl helloImpl = new HelloImpl();
            helloImpl.setORB(orb);
            org.omg.CORBA.Object ref = rootpoa.servant_to_reference(helloImpl);
            Date href = DateHelper.narrow(ref);
            org.omg.CORBA.Object objRef =
                    orb.resolve_initial_references("NameService");
            NamingContextExt ncRef = NamingContextExtHelper.narrow(objRef);
            String name = "Date";
            NameComponent path[] = ncRef.to_name(name);
            ncRef.rebind(path, href);
            System.out.println("HelloServer ready and waiting \ldots{}");
            orb.run();
        } catch (Exception e) {
            System.err.println("ERROR: " + e);
            e.printStackTrace(System.out);
        }
        System.out.println("DateServer Exiting \ldots{}");
    }
}
```

FIGURE 2.9. An example of a simple CORBA server. Code in the shaded area implements Java's CORBA framework.

The Java programming language, however, provides the Remote Method Invocation (RMI) distributed system, based on Modula-3 network objects [14], that allows for the dynamic representation of data and therefore allows for polymorphic data to be transmitted and received across the network [116]. More recently, the Jini distributed system [102] builds on the idea of polymorphic data representation

```
import DateApp.*;
import org.omg.CosNaming.*;
import org.omg.CORBA.*;

public class DateClient {
    static Date dateImpl;

    public static void main(String args[]) {
        try {
            // create and initialize the ORB
            ORB orb = ORB.init(args, null);

            // get the root naming context
            org.omg.CORBA.Object objRef =
                    orb.resolve_initial_references("NameService");
            // Use NamingContextExt instead of NamingContext. This is
            // part of the Interoperable naming Service.
            NamingContextExt ncRef = NamingContextExtHelper.narrow(objRef);

            // resolve the Object Reference in Naming
            String name = "Date";
            dateImpl = DateHelper.narrow(ncRef.resolve_str(name));

            System.out.println("Server's Date: " + dateImpl.getDate());

            dateImpl.shutdown();

        } catch (Exception e) {
            System.out.println("ERROR : " + e);
            e.printStackTrace(System.out);
        }
    }
}
```

FIGURE 2.10. An example of a simple CORBA client. Code in
the shaded area implements Java's CORBA framework.

by allowing for the discovery and spontaneous interaction between services in a
network.

As mentioned in Section 2.3, in order to reduce the programmers' burden,
RPC systems attempt to mask the differences between local and remote procedures
so that a remote procedure call is treated the same as a local procedure call.

Most distributed systems provide a unified view of objects in terms of their
location so that all objects are considered equal regardless of their physical location. Indeed, many distributed systems, including most RPC systems, try and
mask the differences between local and remote objects by providing programmer
transparency.

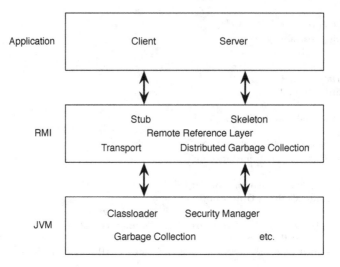

FIGURE 2.11. RMI system architecture.

Waldo et al. [118] argue that this approach is fundamentally wrong and that non-distributed objects cannot be treated the same as distributed objects as there are fundamental differences in terms of latency, memory access, partial failure, and concurrency. They further argue that the merging of the computational models of local and distributed computing is both unwise to attempt and unable to succeed.

Java's Remote Method Invocation (RMI) takes an entirely different approach to other types of distributed systems. RMI differs not only in the details but in the basic set of assumptions made about the distributed systems in which it operates [116].

While most distributed systems are heterogeneous, RMI assumes that the client and the server are both running in a Java virtual machine and are both written in Java. By doing so, RMI removes the need to describe remote interfaces using a language-neutral IDL. Instead, the Java interface construct is used to declare a remotely accessible interface as shown below:

```
public interface IDateService extends java.rmi.Remote {
  Date getDate() throws RemoteException;
}
```

The RMI system architecture is illustrated in Figure 2.11. Messages from the client application to the server pass through the stub (or proxy), an implementation of the remote objects exported interface.

The stub object is generated either statically by the RMI compiler, rmid, or dynamically at runtime. Unlike standard RPC IDL compilers, such as those provided by CORBA systems, the stubs are generated on the implementation class of the object which the stub refers to. These stub objects therefore support all the remote methods that the remote object's implementation supports. In a system such as CORBA, the stub is compiled into the client and linked before runtime. In RMI, the stub originates with the client and is loaded dynamically and may therefore be different for different objects with the same apparent type. The actual type of the stub is loaded at runtime when the system is able to determine the exact type [116].

The stub forwards requests to the server using the remote reference layer. The remote reference layer implements the semantics of the type of invocation, for example unicast or multicast communication. The remote reference layer therefore provides a framework for adding additional types of remote object communication [122], although unicast communication is the only implementation that is provided by default.

The transport layer is responsible for connection setup, connection management and keeping track of and dispatching to remote objects. To dispatch to a remote object, the call is forwarded by the transport to the server specific remote reference layer. The remote reference layer hands the request off to the server's skeleton, which in turn passes it to the remote object implementation to perform the actual method call. Return values from the call are passed back through the skeleton, the remote reference layer, and finally to the client stub [122].

The RMI system passes parameters and return values either by reference or by value. If the object to be passed is a remote object (it implements the `java.rmi.Remote` interface) a remote reference is passed. If, however, the object is not a remote object, a copy of that object is passed.

RMI uses Java's object serialization mechanism to marshal and unmarshal parameters and return values, which encodes objects and any objects they refer to, into a byte stream for transmission from one virtual machine to another. Once the byte stream is received, it is converted into the original object using a process known as de-serialization. RMI therefore requires that all objects and any objects they reference, that are used as parameters or return values, implement the `java.io.Serializable` interface, a marker interface (one that has no methods) that indicates to the serialization system that they may be safely converted to a byte stream.

The objects that are passed are 'real objects' in the sense that they include both the object's data as well as an annotation describing the type of the object. If an object of a previously unknown type is received, the RMI system fetches the bytecode for the object and loads it into the receiving process. By preserving the object's type, RMI preserves the basic object-oriented notion of polymorphism [116, 122].

In order to fetch the bytecode of a previously unknown object, RMI uses Java's dynamic class-loading mechanism. The following classes are loaded during an RMI call [122]:

- Classes of remote objects and their interfaces.
- Stub and skeleton classes that serve as proxies for remote objects.

- Other classes used directly in an RMI application, such as parameters and return values.

The actual location of classes that may be needed to be loaded at runtime are defined by the system property `java.rmi.server.codebase`, a URL pointing to the location of the class files. Classes loaded by RMI are subject to security restrictions put in place by the `java.lang.SecurityManager` class installed for the virtual machine downloading the class. For classes downloaded into applets or applications as a result of remote calls, RMI requires a security manager to protect the application and host from potential harm [122].

Java automatically deletes objects that are no longer referenced. RMI extends this to remote objects by using a reference counting mechanism similar to that used by Modula-3 network objects [14]. RMI implements remote garbage collection by keeping track of all live remote references in all virtual machines. When a remote object is first referenced, a count is incremented and a referenced message is sent to the remote object's RMI runtime. When a live reference is unreferenced, the count is decremented. When the count reaches 0 an unreferenced message is sent to the remote object's RMI runtime, which is then free to garbage-collect the object.

Clients hold references to remote objects for a certain period of time, called a lease. It is the responsibility of the client to automatically renew the lease before it expires. If the lease expires, the server assumes the client is no longer referencing the remote object and is free to garbage-collect it [122]. Using this mechanism it is still possible, however, for a client to call a remote object that has been garbage-collected. For example, if the network is down for a short period of time and the client's RMI runtime could not renew the lease, the client could, upon the network connection being restored, call a remote object that has been garbage-collected. In this instance a `java.rmi.RemoteException` exception is thrown.

RMI uses a simple naming service to bootstrap RMI applications. Servers register remote objects they are exporting with a name server called a registry. When a client wishes to obtain a reference to a remote object, a lookup is performed on a registry and a reference to the remote object is returned if the lookup succeeds.

Registry services can be used by either using the traditional RPC mechanism of a centralised registry or by each application maintaining its own registry.

Because RMI services generally return remote objects, the registry only needs to be contacted when making initial contact with a remote application because once one of the remote objects on a server has been obtained, additional objects can be obtained via method calls on the first object [28].

2.5.1   RMI Example

In order to implement our simple date application, we are firstly required to define the remote interface, illustrated in Figure 2.12, which is required to extend from the `java.rmi.Remote` interface and each remote method is required to declare that it throws the `java.rmi.RemoteException` exception.

```
public interface IDateServer extends Remote {
  public Date getDate() throws RemoteException;
}
```

FIGURE 2.12. RMI interface. RMI requires an interface to be
defined listing the methods that are available to remote clients.

```
public class DateServer implements IDateServer {
    public DateServer() {
        super();
    }

    public Date getDate() throws RemoteException {

        return new Date();
    }
    public static void main(String[] args) {

        if (System.getSecurityManager() == null) {
            System.setSecurityManager(new RMISecurityManager());
        }
        try {

            IdateServer server = new DateServer();

            IdateServer stub =
                (IdateServer) UnicastRemoteObject.exportObject(server, 0);
            Registry registry = LocateRegistry.getRegistry();
            registry.rebind("DateServer", stub);
            System.out.println("Server Ready");
        } catch (RemoteException e) {
            System.err.println("DateServer exception:");
            e.printStackTrace();
        }

    }
}
```

FIGURE 2.13. An example of an RMI server. Code in the shaded
area implements the RMI framework.

To implement our server application we can either extend the
java.rmi.server.UnicastRemoteObject, if we would like the remote object to be
implicitly exported, or we can explicitly export the object using the exportObject
method of the same class.

```
public class DateClient {

    public static void main(String args[]) {

        if (System.getSecurityManager() == null) {
            System.setSecurityManager(new RMISecurityManager());
        }
        try {
            Registry registry = LocateRegistry.getRegistry();
            IDateServer dateServer =
                (IDateServer) registry.lookup("DateServer");
            System.out.println("Date on server: " +

            dateServer.getDate().toString());

        } catch (RemoteException e) {
            System.err.println("DateServer Exception:");
            e.printStackTrace();
        } catch (NotBoundException e) {
            System.err.println("Cannot bind to server");
            e.printStackTrace();
        }

    }
}
```

FIGURE 2.14. An example of an RMI client. Code in the shaded area implements the RMI framework.

In the example in Figure 2.13, our server explicitly exports a remote object, which returns an object of type Date to the client. The date object is serialized into a byte stream and passed to the client application, where it is deserialized and accessed by the client, as shown by the client implementation in Figure 2.14:

As can be seen in our simple example, the RMI framework is highly intrusive as it requires programmers to define an interface that extends the java.rmi.Remote interface (Figure 2.12) and to implement the interface in the server (Figure 2.13) code. The client code, illustrated in Figure 2.14, contains RMI specific code to locate the server and execute the remote method. In addition, the client is required to be aware of the distributed nature of the application by ensuring that it catches a RemoteException exception should one occur.

2.5.2 Summary

RMI provides a sophisticated environment for distributed computing. However, as Hicks et al. [49] point out, programmers need to take special care to distinguish between remote and local method invocation as the argument passing convention between the two are different. As well as argument passing conventions, the `equals()`, `hashCode()`, and `toString()` methods of the `Object` class are overridden by the `java.rmi.RemoteObject` class to deal appropriately with remote objects, for example by displaying information about the transport of the object in the case of the `toString()` method. RMI applications do not, therefore, behave the same as local applications, which adds to the programmer's burden.

The major shortcoming of RMI is that, by ensuring that programmers are aware of the differences between local and remote objects, an additional burden is placed on programmers. While Waldo et al. [118] argue that this is necessary, there are a number of significant issues with RMI's implementation of this approach:

- Programming is far more complicated than the transparent approach adopted by most RPC type systems.
- The programmer has to mark an object as being remote by having it implement the `java.rmi.Remote` interface.
- Remote operations have to be declared to throw the `java.rmi.RemoteException` exception.
- Classes that are marked remote and have operations that are declared to throw `java.rmi.RemoteException` in an interface, have to be altered to be reused outside RMI.
- Clients, and servers that are also clients, are required to provide a security manager to ensure applications can only access resources they are entitled to.
- Applications are required to use the RMI framework for exporting and locating objects.

2.6   Message-Oriented Middleware

Message-oriented middleware (MOM) systems refer to a type of asynchronous communication known as *message queueing* [9] where middleware is commonly defined as a software layer that provides a higher level of abstraction, which considerably simplifies distributed systems development [32]. MOM systems are highly successful in industry and represent a sizeable segment of the Information and Communication Technology market [32].

As described by Eugster et al. [34], MOM systems are generally highly scalable as the decoupling of message producer from consumer improves scalability by removing all explicit dependencies between the interacting participants along the following two dimensions:

Time decoupling. The interacting parties do not need to be actively participating in the interaction at the same time. Either party may be disconnected while the other is sending messages to it. Once they become connected, they may be notified of an event sent by the other party and the other party may be currently disconnected.

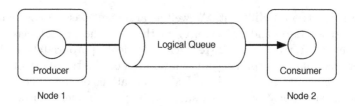

FIGURE 2.15. Message queues.

Space decoupling. The interacting parties do not need to know each other as publishers publish messages through an event service and subscribers receive these events indirectly from the event service. Publishers and subscribers are not aware of each other nor do they hold references to each other.

A number of message queueing systems are widely available, such as MQSeries from IBM [51], Microsoft's MSMQ [25] and Apache's ActiveMQ [5] and message queueing is part of the Java Enterprise Edition (JEE) specification [104] in the form of message-driven beans and the Java Message Service (JMS) API [47].

Message queueing systems typically provide two different interaction styles, queues and publish/subscribe.

2.6.1   Message Queues

In the queue interaction style, also referred to as *point-to-point*, messages are stored in a FIFO queue. Producers append messages into the queue and consumers dequeue them at the front of the queue.

Queues typically provide transactional, ordering and timing guarantees and messages can be one way (fire-and-forget) or two way (request-response) although a response is not compulsory.

The JMS API [47] provides a simple queuing abstraction for Java applications. Implementing our simple date application is therefore straightforward. The server implementation illustrated in Figure 2.16 is developed using Apache's ActiveMQ [5] messaging product.

In our JMS server example we use the JMS `TextMessage` type to pass a String representing the current date from the server to the client. A `Properties` object is used to set various connection parameters required by the JMS implementation and the `DateServer` class is used as a `MessageListener` so that it may receive messages asynchronously.

The JMS Server example uses a simple messaging request-reply pattern [50] where the consumer waits for a message to be sent from the producer and, upon receipt, sends a response back to the producer on a queue defined by the producer in the JMS reply header field. Once a message is received and if it is of type `TextMessage`, the request is printed and a response is sent containing the server's current date. Our client, illustrated in Figure 2.17, creates a temporary queue for

```
public class DateServer implements MessageListener {
    private Queue destination;
    private Session session;

    private void initialize() throws JMSException, NamingException {
        Properties props = new Properties();
        props.setProperty(Context.INITIAL_CONTEXT_FACTORY,
                "org.apache.activemq.jndi.ActiveMQInitialContextFactory");
        props.setProperty(Context.PROVIDER_URL,"tcp://localhost:61616");
        props.setProperty("queue.destination","TEST");
        Context ctx = new InitialContext(props);
        QueueConnectionFactory connectionFactory =
                (QueueConnectionFactory) ctx.lookup("ConnectionFactory");
        QueueConnection c = connectionFactory.createQueueConnection();
        destination = (Queue) ctx.lookup("destination");
        session = c.createQueueSession(false,Session.AUTO_ACKNOWLEDGE);
        MessageConsumer requestConsumer = session.createConsumer(destination);
        requestConsumer.setMessageListener(this);
        c.start();
    }

    public static void main(String[] args) throws NamingException, JMSException {
        new DateServer().initialize();
    }

    public void onMessage(Message message) {
        try {
            if ((message instanceof TextMessage) &&
                    (message.getJMSReplyTo() != null)) {
                TextMessage requestMessage = (TextMessage) message;
                System.out.println("Req Date: " + requestMessage.getText());
                Destination replyDestination = message.getJMSReplyTo();
                MessageProducer replyProducer =
                    session.createProducer(replyDestination);
                TextMessage replyMessage = session.createTextMessage();
                replyMessage.setText(new Date().toString());
                replyMessage.setJMSCorrelationID(requestMessage.
                    getJMSMessageID());
                replyProducer.send(replyMessage);
            }
        } catch (JMSException e) {
            e.printStackTrace();
        }
    }
}
```

FIGURE 2.16. JMS server example. The shaded areas illustrate
where usage of the JMS framework is required.

the receipt of message responses and sets the JMS reply header field to the name
of the temporary queue so that the server knows which queue to use for message
responses. Once a message is sent, the client suspends waiting for a response from
the server.

As can be seen in Figures 2.16 and 2.17, the programmer is responsible for
implementing all aspects of error recovery. In addition, as illustrated by the shad-

```
public class DateClient {

    private Queue destination;
    private Session session;
    private MessageProducer producer;
    private MessageConsumer consumer;
    private Queue replyQueue;

    public static void main(String[] args) throws JMSException, NamingException {

        DateClient d = new DateClient();
        d.initialize();
        System.out.println("Server's Date: " + d.getDate());
        System.exit(0);
    }

    private String getDate() throws JMSException {
        TextMessage requestMessage = session.createTextMessage();
        requestMessage.setText(new Date().toString());
        requestMessage.setJMSReplyTo(replyQueue);
        producer.send(requestMessage);
        Message message = (TextMessage) consumer.receive();
        if (message instanceof TextMessage)
            return ((TextMessage) message).getText();
        return "Invalid Message type Received";
    }

    private void initialize() throws JMSException, NamingException {
        Properties props = new Properties();
        props.setProperty(Context.INITIAL_CONTEXT_FACTORY,
                "org.apache.activemq.jndi.ActiveMQInitialContextFactory");
        props.setProperty(Context.PROVIDER_URL, "tcp://localhost:61616");
        props.setProperty("queue.destination", "TEST");
        Context ctx = new InitialContext(props);
        QueueConnectionFactory connectionFactory =
                (QueueConnectionFactory) ctx.lookup("ConnectionFactory");
        QueueConnection c = connectionFactory.createQueueConnection();
        destination = (Queue) ctx.lookup("destination");
        session = c.createQueueSession(false,Session.AUTO_ACKNOWLEDGE);
        producer = session.createProducer(destination);
        replyQueue = session.createTemporaryQueue();
        consumer = session.createConsumer(replyQueue);
        c.start();
    }
}
```

FIGURE 2.17. JMS client example. The shaded areas illustrate where usage of the JMS framework is required.

ing in the JMS examples, the JMS framework is highly intrusive, requiring a great deal of setup and recovery code.

2.6.2   Publish/Subscribe

In contrast to the synchronous models of communication described earlier, publish/subscribe systems provide a loosely-coupled interaction style where publish-

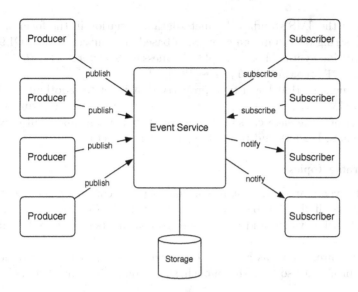

FIGURE 2.18. Publish/subscribe overview.

ers publish events and subscribers subscribe to those events and are subsequently asynchronously notified when an event occurs. Publish/subscribe systems therefore implement an *event-driven* style of communication [78].

This interaction style is illustrated in Figure 2.18, where publishers publish messages to a central event service. Subscribers register their interest in messages that may be placed in the event service by publishers and are notified asynchronously if this occurs.

As well as *time* and *space* decoupling, described in Section 2.6, publish/-subscribe also provides *synchronisation* decoupling between publishers and subscribers. Eugster et al. [34] describe *synchronisation decoupling* as the ability for publishers to produce events without blocking and subscribers to receive those events asynchronously through a callback mechanism.

Subscribers are usually only interested in particular events, not all events and this has led to a number of subscription schemes. According to Eugster et al. [34], the most widely used schemes are *topic-based* and *content-based* subscription.

The topic based subscription model is based on the notion of *topics* or *subjects* and is implemented by many enterprise messaging solutions including IBM's MQ Series [51] and Tibco's Rendezvous message bus [78]. The JMS API [47] provides a topic abstraction mechanism and in version 1.1 of the standard, the interface between message queues and topics has converged so the API for both types of interaction styles are the same. Topic based publish/subscribe programming is, using the JMS API, the same as message queue programming.

Content-based (also known as *property-based* [87]) publish/subscribe provides a scheme where events are subscribed to, based on a filter mechanism. This is implemented in the JMS standard by meta-data association in the form of *message selectors*, a string containing an expression based on a subset of the SQL92 conditional expression syntax. For example, the message selector:

```
Type = 'Football' OR Type = 'Rugby'
```

selects any message that has a type property that is set to 'Football' or 'Rugby'.

In the JMS API, a message selector may be passed as an argument during the creation of a message consumer and the message consumer will only receive messages whose headers and properties match the selector.

2.6.3   Durable Topics

By default, events are only sent to consumers if the consumer is currently available. However, if the durable property is defined, then events are stored in the publish/subscribe system and will be sent to consumers once they become available.

This feature, known as *durable topics*, requires the programmer to define two additional properties so that the publish/subscribe system may uniquely identify a consumer:

- A client ID for the connection so that the system may have many different durable consumers on different topics or on the same topic with different message selectors.
- A subscription name for the consumer.

2.7   Chapter Summary

This chapter has discussed four common approaches to distributed systems development which are broadly indicative of current distributed systems development practises. We classify these approaches as follows:

1. The low-level API approach, which accesses the low-level protocol stack directly.
2. The RPC distribution obliviousness approach, which attempts to hide the distributed system from the programmer.
3. The RPC distribution awareness approach, which ensures the programmer is aware of the distributed nature of the application and requires the programmer to follow specific programming conventions.
4. The high-level framework or API approach, which provides a high-level library or framework that is used to hide low-level networking details from the programmer.

BSD sockets are indicative of the first approach and provide low-level access to the networking stack and therefore greater control, but requires significantly more code than other approaches. Programmers are required to implement their own protocol on top of the socket interface and are responsible for implementing their own packet assembly and disassembly routines. In addition, BSD socket programmers cannot rely on the underlying transport mechanism to ensure message delivery. Error handling and recovery is left entirely up to the programmer, which, combined with the other requirements discussed above, makes socket programming immensely complex and error prone.

Using the second approach, RPC systems attempt to mask the differences between local and remote procedure calls so that, to the programmer, they appear identical. While this approach has its advantages, remote procedure calls do not behave in the same way as local procedure calls, and in the event of an error it is often impossible to recover unless the programmer is aware of the distributed nature of the application and is therefore in a position to take corrective action, for example by reconnecting to a different server. In addition, programmers are required to use an IDL for most RPC type systems, which is used to describe the remote procedure calls, their parameters and other information. An IDL is unique to a distributed system and a programmer is therefore required to learn an additional IDL for each type of RPC system they wish to use.

RMI, an implementation of the third approach, is a Java-centric distributed system that requires the programmer to adopt RMI specific programming conventions. Programmers are required to be aware of the distributed nature of their applications so that they may take corrective action in the event of failures, although there is no specific or general recovery mechanism in the RMI system, rather it is left to the programmer to implement one.

The JMS system uses the fourth approach to provide a high-level API to asynchronous event-driven systems. Once again, error handling and recovery is left to the programmer to resolve.

All of the above approaches require programmers to adhere to a framework or API although the level of abstraction may differ. Regardless of the approach used, programmers are required to interact with the framework or API at some level, thereby tying the application code to the framework or API.

Autonomics Development: A Domain-Specific Aspect Language Approach, 41–66
Book Series: Autonomic Systems
© 2010 Springer Basel AG

3 An Aspect-Oriented Approach

3.1 Introduction

Object-orientation has been presented as the technology that will finally make software reuse a reality as the object model provides a better fit with domain models than procedural programming [63]. Object-orientation, currently the dominant programming paradigm, allows a programmer to build a system by decomposing a problem domain into objects that contain both data and the methods used to manipulate the data, thereby providing both abstraction and encapsulation. In addition, object-oriented languages typically provide an *inheritance* mechanism that allows an object to reuse the data and methods of its parent, thereby enabling polymorphism.

There are, however, many programming problems where the object-oriented programming (OOP) technique, or the procedural programming technique it replaces, are not sufficient to capture the important design decisions a program needs to implement. Kiczales et al. [59] refer to these design decisions as *aspects* and claim the reason they are so difficult to capture is because they crosscut the systems basic functionality. Kiczales et al. claim that AOP makes it possible to clearly express programs involving such aspects, including appropriate isolation, composition and reuse of the aspect code.

3.2 Crosscutting Concerns and Aspects

Separation of concerns has long been a guiding principle of software engineering as it allows one to identify, encapsulate and manipulate only those parts of software that are relevant to a particular goal or purpose [79]. Unfortunately, there can be many concerns that crosscut one another leading to tangled code that is difficult to understand, reuse and evolve. Concerns are said to crosscut if the methods related to those concerns intersect [31] as illustrated in the UML for a simple picture editor[1] in Figure 3.1.

Figure 3.1 illustrates two implementations of the `FigureElement` interface, `Point` and `Line`. Although these classes exhibit good modularity, consider the concern that the screen manager must be notified whenever a `FigureElement` moves. In this case every time a `FigureElement` changes, the screen manager must

---

[1]This example is reproduced from Kiczales et al. [60].

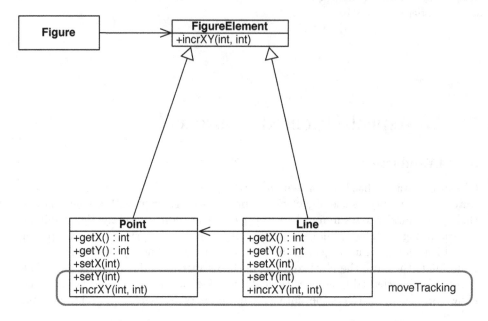

FIGURE 3.1. Aspects crosscut classes in a simple figure editor.

be informed by calling the screen manager's `moveTracking` method, as illustrated by the band surrounding the methods that implements this concern in Figure 3.1. This concern is called a *crosscutting concern* as it crosscuts methods in both the `Line` and the `Point` classes.

AOP is an attempt to isolate and modularise these concerns and then weave or compose them together with an existing program, thereby allowing the concern to be applied in an oblivious way (the existing code is unaware of the crosscutting concern). An aspect can therefore be considered as a modular unit of crosscutting implementation [61].

It is important to note that the goal for AOP is not as a replacement for object-orientation, it is to build on object-orientation by supporting separation of concerns that cannot be adequately expressed in object-oriented languages [31].

3.3   AOP Semantics

AOP introduces new semantics to describe crosscutting concerns and aspects. Much of the semantic model is based on the AspectJ language developed by Kiczales et al. [59] at Xerox's Palo Alto Research Centre.

According to Kiczales et al. [59], aspect-oriented languages have three critical elements: a join point model, a means of identifying join points, and a means of effecting implementation at join points. These elements can be described as:

Join points. A join point model makes it possible to define the structure of cross-cutting concerns. Join points are well-defined points in the execution flow of a program [59], such as method calls, constructors, function calls etc. Join points can therefore be considered as places in a program where aspects may be applied.

Pointcuts. A pointcut is a means used to identify a join point. This is typically a filter mechanism that defines a subset of join points [59]. A `cflow` is a type of pointcut that identifies join points based on whether they occur in the dynamic context of other join points. For example, the `cflow` statement `cflow(move())` in the AspectJ language picks out each join point that occurs between when the `move()` method is called and when it returns, which may occur multiple times in the case of a recursive call [6].

Advice. The advice is used to define additional code that is run at join points. In most AOP languages there are a number of different advice declarations that define when the advice runs when a join point is reached. These are typically before, after, or around the join point.

Weaving. The process of adding aspects to existing code to produce a coherent program is known as *weaving*. Weaving is either done at compile time (static weaving) or at runtime (dynamic weaving) and some systems, such as composition filters [12], allow aspects to be added and removed dynamically. Weaving is achieved using a technique known as bytecode rewriting, which alters existing bytecode, either dynamically as it is loaded or statically by altering the bytecode contained in an existing class file.

As well as the above general AOP semantics, various aspect implementations provide their own semantics.

3.4 Static and Dynamic Weaving

Static weaving refers to the modification of the source code of a class by inserting aspect-specific statements at join points [21]. Java applications are compiled to bytecode, a portable format that is interpreted by the Java virtual machine at runtime, and consequently most Java AOP systems alter the bytecode, not the source code. This has the added advantage of allowing Java AOP systems to be used where the source code is not available.

Dynamic weaving refers to the ability to weave and unweave aspects at runtime without having to restart the application [84].

A number of methods have been proposed to implement aspect-oriented functionality. These can be broadly classified as language-based implementations, framework-based implementations and domain-specific language implementations.

3.5   Language-Based Implementations

A number of language-based approaches have been proposed to implement aspect-oriented programming. Many of these languages, such as AspectJ [60], Caesar [71], Jiazzi [68], AspectC [20], and JAsCo [106] have been designed as extensions to existing languages. Other novel language-based concepts, such as composition filters that manipulate the messages passing between objects, have also been proposed [12].

These languages and systems have typically been produced by the research community attempting to understand the practical value of AOP in terms of how aspects are used, the types of designs and patterns that may emerge, and how effective crosscutting modularity actually is [60]. The most popular language-based system is currently AspectJ.

3.5.1   AspectJ

AspectJ is an extension to the Java programming language that was developed by Kiczales et al. [59] at Xerox's Palo Alto Research Centre. The AspectJ language is designed to be a simple and practical aspect-oriented extension to the Java language that can be used to code crosscutting concerns that would otherwise lead to tangled code [60].

AspectJ is designed as a compatible extension to Java where compatibility is defined by Kiczales et al. [60] as:

- *Upward compatibility* – all legal Java programs are legal AspectJ programs.
- *Platform compatibility* – all legal AspectJ programs must run on standard Java virtual machines.
- *Tool Compatibility* – all existing tools, including IDEs, documentation tools, and design tools should be able to be extended to support AspectJ.
- *Programmer compatibility* – programming in AspectJ must feel like a natural extension to programming in Java.

While early versions of AspectJ operated on source code, later versions alter the bytecode generated by the Java compiler, thereby allowing aspects to be used in situations where the source code is not available.

As discussed in Section 3.3 join points are well-defined points in the execution flow of a program. AspectJ supports a number of join points as listed in Table 3.1 [60].

A pointcut in AspectJ is a set of join points that may be matched at runtime. For example, the pointcut[2]:

```
call(void Point.setX(int)) ||
call(void Point.setY(int))
```

---

[2]These examples are reproduced from Kiczales et al. [60, 61].

TABLE 3.1. The dynamic join points of AspectJ.

Kind of join point	Points in the program execution at which ...
method call constructor call	A method (or a constructor of a class) is called. Call join points are in the calling object, or in no object if the call is from a static method.
method call reception constructor call reception	An object receives a method or constructor call. Reception join points are before method or constructor dispatch, i.e. they happen inside the called object, at a point in the control flow after control has been transferred to the called object, but before any particular method or constructor has been called.
method execution constructor execution	An individual method or constructor is invoked.
field get	A field of an object, class or interface is read.
field set	A field of an object or class is set.
exception handler execution	An exception handler is invoked.
class initialisation	Static initialisers for a class are run.
object initialisation	When the dynamic initialisers for a class are run during object creation.

matches any call to either the `setX` or `setY` methods defined by `Point` that return `void` and have a parameter of `int`. Pointcuts may also be declared by name, for example:

```
pointcut weAreMoving():
    call(void Point.setX(int)) ||
    call(void Point.setY(int));
```

As well as pointcuts that match an explicit method call, as described above, pointcuts may also contain *wildcard* characters that can match a number of different methods. Consider the following:

```
call (public String Figure.get*(..))
call (public * Figure.*(..))
```

The first matches any call to public methods defined in `Figure` that start with `get`, take any number of parameters, and return a `String`. The second matches any call to a public method defined in `Figure`.

AspectJ defines the *advice* declaration to stipulate the code that is run at a join point. Three types of advice are supported:

```
aspect SimpleTracing {
  pointcut traced() :
    call(void Display.update()) ||
    call(void Display.repaint(..));

    before(): traced() {
      println("Entering: " + thisJoinPoint);
    }

    void println(String s) {
      // write message
    }
}
```

FIGURE 3.2. AspectJ SimpleTracing Example.

- *Before* advice – runs at the moment a join point is reached.
- *After* advice – runs after the join point has been reached.
- *Around* advice – runs when the join point is reached and has explicit control over whether the method is run or not.

An advice is declared using one of the advice keywords. For example, the following advice prints a message after the weAreMoving method is called using the after keyword:

```
after(): weAreMoving() {
  System.out.println("We have moved");
}
```

Aspects wrap up pointcuts, advice, and inter-type declarations in a modular unit of crosscutting implementation and is defined similar to a class. Inter-type declarations are members of an aspect (fields, members and constructors) that are owned by other types, and aspects can also declare that other types implement new interfaces or extend a new class [6].

Aspects can contain methods, fields, and initialisers in addition to the cross-cutting members. The following is an example of a simple aspect that is used to print messages before certain display operations:

As can be seen from the example in Figure 3.2, aspects in AspectJ are not reusable because the context on which an aspect needs to be deployed is specified directly in the aspect definition – the pointcut is part of the aspect [106]. Although AspectJ allows aspects to be inherited from other aspects, it is only allowed if the inherited aspect has been declared as *abstract*. Concrete aspects are therefore not reusable. In addition, any change to a class may result in the necessity to alter the aspect as the pointcut definition may no longer be valid.

Recognising this limitation, a number of researchers have been focusing on removing the join point interception model from the aspect implementation. Lieberherr et al. [64] have developed the concept of Aspectual Components, which attempts to separate the pointcut from the advice, thereby making the advice reusable. This method has subsequently been adopted by Suvée et al. [106] in the JAsCo language. The Caesar system [71], uses an *aspect collaboration interface*, a higher-level module concept that decouples the aspect implementation from the aspect bindings, to enable reuse and componentisation of aspects.

As well as providing aspects, AspectJ also provides *introductions*, a mechanism for adding fields, methods and interfaces to existing classes. Introductions are motivated by the observation that concerns have an impact on the type structure of programs which compromises modularisation, because different fields and methods in the type structure may come from different concerns. With introductions, these fields and methods can be removed from the various concerns, modularised, and applied to the various classes at runtime [46].

3.6 Framework-Based Implementations

One approach to the implementation of AOP is by providing an object-oriented framework [80], a reusable semi-complete application that can be specialised to produce custom applications [55]. A framework dictates the architecture of an application by [41]:

- Defining its overall structure.
- Partitioning the application into classes and objects.
- Defining the key responsibilities of the classes and objects.
- Dictating how the classes and objects collaborate.
- Defining the application's thread of control.

These design parameters are predefined so that an application programmer can concentrate on the specifics of the application and not on the architecture [41].

The important classes in a framework are usually abstract. An abstract class is a class with no instances and is used only as a superclass [36]. As well as providing an interface, an abstract class provides part of the implementation of its subclasses by using either a template method or a hook method. A template method defines part of the implementation in an abstract class and defers other parts to subclasses by calling methods that are defined as abstract [41]. A hook method defines a default implementation that can be overridden by subclasses [86]. Abstract classes that are intended to be subclassed by the framework user are known as hot spots as they encapsulate possible variations [85].

Frameworks usually come with a component library containing concrete subclasses of the abstract classes in the framework [36]. According to Fayad et al. [36], frameworks provide the following benefits:

Modularity. Implementation details are hidden behind stable interfaces. This helps to improve quality by localising the impact of design and implementation changes.

```
1   public class MyAspect {
2     public Object trace(MethodInvocation invocation)
3           throws Throwable {
4       try {
5         System.out.println("Entering method");
6         // proceed to next advice or actual call
7         return invocation.invokeNext();
8       } finally {
9         System.out.println("Leaving method");
10      }
11    }
12  }
```

FIGURE 3.3. JBoss aspect example.

Reusability. The stable interfaces provided by frameworks define generic compo-
    nents that can be reused in new applications.
Extensibility. A framework provides hook methods that can be re-implemented by
    subclasses.
Inversion of control. This allows the framework, as opposed to the application, to
    decide which application specific methods to invoke in response to external
    events.

Frameworks are designed to either be used as a general purpose framework
usable in any environment, such as AspectWerkz [16], or to be used in a specific
environment, such as the JEE framework. Components that have been developed
to a specific framework environment cannot be reused outside that environment,
severely limiting reuse.

3.6.1   The JBoss AOP Framework

The JBoss AOP framework provides a framework that can be used to develop
aspect-oriented applications that are either tightly coupled to the JBoss JEE application server or are standalone. To use the framework, the programmer defines
AOP constructs as Java classes and binds them to application code using XML or
Java 1.5 annotations [54].

Aspect classes are defined as normal Java class that define zero or more advices, pointcuts and/or mixins (a mixin class is a class that is used to implement
multiple unrelated interfaces and is often used as an alternative to multiple inheritance [17]).

Figure 3.3 contains an example of an aspect called MyAspect[3], which contains
an advice, trace (line two), that traces calls to any method. The return statement,
invocation.invokeNext() (line seven) is **required** in order to ensure that either

---

[3]All examples presented in this section are reproduced from: *JBoss AOP – Aspect-Oriented
Framework for Java* [54].

TABLE 3.2. Pointcuts supported by JBoss AOP.

Pointcut Type	Description
execution(method or constructor)	Specifies that an interception occurs whenever a specified method or constructor is called.
get(field expression)	Specifies that an interception occurs when a specified field is accessed to be read.
set(field expression) field	Specifies that an interception occurs when a specified field is accessed to be written to.
field(field expression)	Specifies that an interception occurs when a specified field is accessed to be read from or written to.
all(type expression)	Specifies that calls to a specified constructor, method or field of a particular class will be intercepted.
call(method or constructor)	Specifies that calls to a specified constructor or method will be intercepted.
within(type expression)	Matches any join point (method or constructor call) within any code within a particular call.
withincode(method or constructor)	Matches any join point (method or constructor call) within a particular method or constructor.
has(method or constructor)	Used as an additional requirement for matching. If a join point is matched, its class must also have a constructor or method that matches the **has** expression.
hasfield(field expression)	Used as an additional requirement for matching. If a join point is matched, its class must also have a constructor or method that matches the **hasfield** expression.

the next advice in the chain (if there is more than one) or the actual method or constructor invocation is called. Failure to adhere to this protocol results in the failure to call other advice and/or the method or constructor.

The framework also supports other invocation types such as all invocations, `public Object trace(Invocation invocation)`, and constructor invocations, `public Object trace(ConstructorInvocation invocation)`.

XML files are used by the framework to describe pointcuts and the attachment of pointcuts to aspects. Table 3.2 lists the types of pointcuts supported by the JBoss AOP framework [54].

For example, the XML constructs used to trace all calls to the `withdraw` method on any object that has a parameter of `double` using the `MyAspect` aspect example presented in Figure 3.3 is:

```
<aop>
  <aspect class="MyAspect"/>
  <bind pointcut=
     "execution(* void *->withdraw(double amount))">
     <advice name="trace" aspect="MyAspect"/>
  </bind>
</aop>
```

One of the more interesting features of the JBoss AOP framework is that it allows for the use of *introductions* and *mixins*. An introduction is used to alter an existing class so that it implements one or more additional interfaces. For example the class:

```
public class POJO {
  private String field;
}
```

can be made to implement the `java.io.Externalizable` interface by using the following XML:

```
<introduction class="POJO">
   <mixin>
      <interfaces>
         java.io.Externalizable
      </interfaces>
      <class>ExternalizableMixin</class>
      <construction>
         new ExternalizableMixin(this)
      </construction>
   </mixin>
</introduction>
```

The class element above defines the mixin class that will implement the externalizable interface, while the construction element specifies the Java code that will be used to initialise the mixin class when it is created.

The JBoss AOP framework also has the ability to allow the deployment and undeployment of aspects at runtime. This is achieved by using the `aopc` compiler to 'prepare' join points in the application to accept advices at runtime. Preparing alters the bytecode by inserting dummy placeholders where advice can later be applied [54].

The JBoss AOP framework is an extensive elegant framework that supports many complex AOP constructs as well as many useful features, such as the hot deployment/undeployment of aspects at runtime. As with many object-oriented frameworks it requires the programmer to adhere to a specified protocol, such as ensuring that the `invocation.invokeNext()` method is called in an aspect. If the programmer fails to adhere to this protocol, the application will not behave as expected. Unfortunately these types of issues can only be picked up at runtime, not compile time.

TABLE 3.3.   Four aspects of self-management with autonomic computing.

Concept	Current Computing	Autonomic Computing
Self-configuration	Corporate data centres have multiple vendors and platforms. Installing, configuring, and integrating systems is time consuming and error prone.	Automated configuration of components and systems follows high-level policies. Rest of system adjusts automatically and seamlessly.
Self-optimisation	Systems have hundreds of manually set, nonlinear tuning parameters, and their number increases with each release.	Components and systems continually seek opportunities to improve their own performance and efficiency.
Self-healing	Problem determination in large, complex systems can take a team of programmers weeks.	System automatically detects, diagnoses, and repairs localised software and hardware problems.
Self-protection	Detection of and recovery from attacks and cascading failures is manual.	System automatically defends against malicious attacks or cascading failures. It uses early warning to anticipate and prevent systemwide failures.

3.7   AOP and Autonomics

Autonomic computing is an initiative proposed by the IBM corporation to overcome an impending complexity crisis in the development of applications [52]. According to IBM, this complexity is growing beyond human ability to manage it.

To overcome this, IBM proposes that systems are developed to manage themselves, given high-level objectives by administrators, so that they may adjust their operation, workloads, demands and external conditions in the face of hardware or software failures. IBM cites four aspects of self-management, which are detailed in Table 3.3 [56].

To meet the autonomic computing vision of self-managing, self-healing and self-optimising systems requires a system to be able to dynamically adapt to its environment. However, a key challenge limiting the use of autonomic features in applications is the lack of tools and frameworks that can alleviate the complexities stemming from the use of manual development methods [56].

McKinley et al. [69] define two general approaches to implement adaptive software:

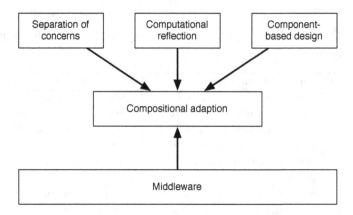

FIGURE 3.4. Main technologies supporting compositional adaption.

Parameter adaption modifies program variables that are used to determine behaviour, for example by adjusting a retry count depending on current network conditions. This type of adaption is severely limited as it does not allow new algorithms and software components to be added to an application after initial design and development.

Compositional adaption allows an application to replace parts of a program's components with another to improve the program's fit into the current operating environment, for example by adding new behaviour to a deployed system. While this is much more flexible than parameter adaption, incorrect use may result in a program that is difficult to test and debug.

McKinley et al. [69] define three main technologies, illustrated in Figure 3.4[4], that can be used to support compositional adaption; *separation of concerns*, *computational reflection*, and *component-based design*.

There are two main techniques used to implement compositional adaption in application code. The first is to use a language, such as CLOS or Python, that directly supports dynamic recomposition, and the second is to weave the adaptive code into the functional code using aspect-oriented techniques [69].

For the purposes of this discussion we concentrate on using the AOP technique to develop adaptive software and present relevant implementations of this approach.

---

[4]This diagram is reproduced from McKinley et al. [69].

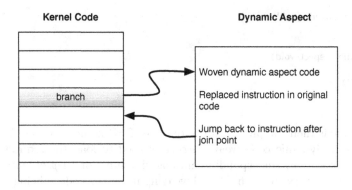

FIGURE 3.5. TOSKANA Code Splicing.

3.7.1   The TOSKANA Toolkit

Engel and Freisleben [33] have developed the TOSKANA toolkit to dynamically apply aspects to the NetBSD operating system. This toolkit provides a set of tools, macros and libraries for developing and deploying dynamic aspects in the kernel space of NetBSD.

Aspects are developed using standard C macros and are inserted into the kernel as loadable kernel modules. A runtime library, called *aspectlib.ko*, dynamically applies join points using a technique known as *code splicing*. Code splicing replaces the bit patterns of instructions in native code with a branch to a location outside the predefined code flow, where additional instructions followed by the originally replaced instruction and a jump back to the instruction after the splicing location are inserted. As the execution of kernel functions may usually be interrupted at any time, the splicing operation is performed atomically [33]. This process is illustrated in Figure 3.5[5].

TOSKANA supports **before**, **after** and **around** advice variants and these are implemented using the BEFORE, AFTER and AROUND macros in standard C code as illustrated below:

```
#include <sys/aspects.h>
...
void aspect_init(void) { /* deploy three aspects */
    BEFORE(sys_open, open_aspect);
    AFTER(sys_open, close_aspect);
    AROUND(func, some_aspect);
}
ASPECT open_aspect(void) {
    ...
}
```

---

[5]This diagram is reproduced from Engel and Freisleben [33].

```
ASPECT close_aspect(void) {
    ...
}
ASPECT some_aspect(void) {
    ...
    PROCEED();
    ...
}
```

The code is then compiled as a standard NetBSD kernel module. At runtime, the user mode dynamic code weaver *weave* is used to load the requested kernel module and execute its corresponding initialisation function (*aspect_init()*), which calls a support library to do the actual weaving using the code splicing technique. Subsequent functions calls are then routed through the user-provided aspects.

Engel and Freisleben [33] provide a number of use cases of adding adaption to NetBSD using this approach:

Self-Configuration. In common with most operating systems, new devices may be added or removed from the NetBSD operating system dynamically. While adding a new device does not affect running processes, removing one may. For example removing a USB memory key that contains a file system that is currently being accessed by a process. The cross-cutting functionality affected here is the call to the *VOP_OPEN* function, located in 43 areas in the architecture-specific, base kernel, file system and device driver code in the operating system. In this scenario an aspect may intercept the device removal and signal the different parts of the operating system affected that a device is no longer available if the operating system tries to open a file on the now non-existent device.

Self-Healing. The NetBSD system, in common with all operating systems, may run out of memory if a process requests more memory than that which is available in the virtual memory system. Using an aspect, the out-of-memory error condition can be intercepted and the aspect can add additional virtual memory dynamically by adding additional swap files to the system.

Self-Optimization. To calculate the number of free blocks in a file system, the operating system skims through the free block list and counts the number of bits that indicate a free block. However, if the operating system could detect that reading the free block count occurs more frequently than updating the free block bitmap, an optimisation could be achieved by dynamically switching the free block calculation so that the number of free blocks is calculated prior to every bitmap update instead of every call to a readout. This provides self optimisation because the system can dynamically shift the count of free blocks depending on changing conditions and this functionality can be provided in an aspect.

```
behavior RSSBehavior()
{                                                               ──── Method
  //Instance variable declarations...
  octet[] examples::bette::SlideShow.:read (in long gifNumber)
  {
     return_value octet[] result;
     local instr::Trace_rec rec;

     after METHODENTRY {                                        ──── Join Point
       methodID = "read";
       rec = rssQosket.createTraceRec(methodID);               ──── Advice
     }
     inplaceof METHODCALL {
       region slow {                                            ──── Region
        java_code #{
          iServer =
          (com.bbn.quo.examples.bette.SlideShowInstrumented)
            rssQosket.getInstrumentedServer();                      Advice
        }#;
        instrumented_result = iServer.read(gifNumber,rec);
        result = instrumented_result.getBytes();
        rec = instrnmented_result.getRecord();
       }
     }
  }
};
```

FIGURE 3.6. QuO ASL example.

This approach presents the possibility of operating systems being able to be modularised to a far greater extent than that which is currently possible and, as described above, provides the possibly to add autonomic computing functionality.

3.7.2 The QuO Toolkit

Middleware technologies, such as CORBA [77], allow the development of distributed applications without the developer needing to be aware of details of the distribution technology involved. As these applications may be distributed across a number of different physical machines connected via one or more networks, the applications concerned may need to adapt to the changing network and system conditions to maintain an acceptable quality of of service (QoS).

Duzan et al. [30] have developed the QuO toolkit which builds QoS as an aspect and weaves the aspect into the boundary between the application and the middleware. QoU defines an aspect model, which includes join points specific to distribution and adaption, and an adaption model which defines the adaption strategy to be used. The QuO toolkit consists of four main entities [30]:

1. Contracts, which are used to define an adaption policy in QuO. Contracts are defined using QUO's Contract Definition Language (CDL).
2. System Condition Objects, which are used to monitor the environment.

3. Callbacks, which are used for system, middleware and out-of-band application adaption.
4. Delegates, which define the aspect-oriented weaving of the adaptive behaviour into wrappers around application interfaces.

QuO provides an Aspect Specification Language (ASL), which is used to define the monitoring or control behaviour and is compiled to produce a *delegate*, which acts as a proxy for calls to an object reference or a servent (the remote object).

Figure 3.6 illustrates an example of QuO's ASL used to define two advices that are to be applied for the method `examples::bette::SlideShow::read`.

Although delegates may be defined for other middleware environments, the current implementation of the QuO toolkit is designed for the CORBA environment and therefore the ASL advice is applied to a particular method in the CORBA IDL, e.g. `examples::bette::SlideShow::read` in Figure 3.6.

The region statement in the ASL Figure 3.6 refers to a region defined in QuO's Contract Definition Language (not shown), which defines the meaning of the term 'slow'. In this example, once the system reaches that state, the corresponding advice is executed.

3.7.3   Reflection and AOP

A reflective system is a system that incorporates structures about itself. The sum of these structures is called the self-representation of the system, which makes it possible for the system to answer questions about itself and support actions on its behalf [67].

In a language that supports reflection, each object is given a *meta-object*, which holds the reflective information available about the object [67]. Metaobject protocols (MOP's) are interfaces, to the language that give users the ability to incrementally modify the language's behaviour and implementation [58], typically by using a set of classes and methods that allow a program to inspect and alter the state of the application.

Reflection is a common way of developing adaptive software and Grace et al. [43] have proposed combining the use of AOP and reflective middleware to implement dynamic adaptive systems to provide the following benefits:

- The ability to support fine-grained introspection and dynamic adaption of aspects including the ability to adapt or re-order advice behaviour and re-configure the joinpoint set thereby supporting self-adaption and system wide validation of crosscutting concerns.
- The provision of multiple system viewpoints to support complex adaptions. For example an MOP to manage component adaption, another to manage crosscutting module adaption and another to manage resource usage adaption.

- Increased performance (compared to a purely reflective implementation) by deploying reflection using aspects only where required.

Surajbali et al. [105] argue that the reflective middleware approach is limiting as the reflective APIs have been found to expose a steep learning curve and places too much expressive power in the hands of developers. Instead their approach is to build an AOP support layer on top of an underlying component-based reflective middleware substrate. Surajbali et al. [105] provide an implementation of their model using the OpenCOM component model and the GridKit middleware platform and claim their approach provides the following benefits [105]:

- The complexity of the reflection layer is hidden from programmers.
- The AOP support layer can be dynamically deployed and undeployed when required thereby avoiding overhead when not in use.
- As the AOP support layer is constructed from OpenCOM components like the rest of the system, the underlying middleware system and the AOP support layer can be the target of an advice.
- As distributed dynamic aspects are supported, aspects can be dynamically deployed across a distributed system on the basis of distributed pointcut expressions.

Greenwood and Blair [44] have proposed the use of *dynamic AOP* to implement autonomics. This approach allows adaptions to be encapsulated as aspects, thereby allowing adaptions to be contained and applied retrospectively at runtime.

Greenwood and Blair's implementation [45] uses the AspectWerkz [16] dynamic AOP framework combined with reflection and a policy framework to define adaptive behaviour based on Event-Condition-Action rules.

3.8 AOP and the Distribution Concern

Several attempts have been made to apply distribution aspects to existing Java code. These attempts typically target a single distribution protocol, RMI, and either generate code in the general purpose aspect language, AspectJ [18, 91, 114], use a domain-specific language [66, 73], extend Java [83], or extend the AspectJ language to provide distribution [74].

While RMI is the most widely used distribution protocol in Java systems and is used as the protocol for Enterprise JavaBeans (EJB), Jini and JavaSpaces, there are a number of other distributed systems, such as CORBA, JMS, SOAP, HTTP, Java sockets etc. that Java programmers may choose to use and indeed may have to use to solve a particular integration problem.

Programmers therefore have a large choice of protocols, each with its own framework and possibly different programming convention. This significantly complicates distributed systems development.

3.8.1   Domain-Specific Aspect Language Implementations

We define a domain-specific aspect language as a language designed for a specific domain e. g. distribution, that is used by an aspect weaver to insert code based on instructions and possibly code contained in the language into existing code either statically, at compile time, or dynamically at runtime.

A number of domain-specific aspect languages have been proposed including KALA for the transactional domain [35], ERTSAL for the real-time domain [94] and ALPH for the healthcare domain [72].

Many domain-specific languages (e. g. Orca [8]) have been proposed to aid distributed programming, and seminal work on aspect-orientation proposes a number of domain-specific aspect languages, such as the D language framework consisting of the domain-specific aspect languages COOL, for concurrency management, and RIDL for distribution [66], and the RG language [70], amongst others.

Since the RIDL language was conceived, little work has been done on domain-specific aspect languages for the distribution concern and the closest work to ours thus far are RIDL and AWED, which we describe in this section.

3.8.1.1   The D Language Framework

The D language framework consists of three sub-languages:

- JCore, an object-oriented language used to express the basic functionality and the activity of the system. JCore is a subset of Java 1.0.
- COOL, an aspect language used to express the co-ordination of threads.
- RIDL, an aspect language used to express distribution and remote access strategies.

A tool that implements an aspect weaver takes the programs written in the different sub-languages and combines them to produce an executable program with the specified distributed behaviour. The D framework consists of three types of modules [65]:

- Classes – Used to implement functional components.
- Coordinators – Used to implement the thread coordination aspect.
- Portals – Used to define code for dealing with application-level data transfers over remote method invocations.

For the purposes of this discussion, we concentrate on RIDL, the aspect language used to express remote access strategies.

RIDL is used to define remote RMI objects, the parameter passing mode for each distributed method in those objects, and the parts of the object graph that should be copied if the call uses the copy-by-value semantics.

In order for an object to become a remote object, RIDL requires that a remote interface and portal be defined (for that object) that stipulates the subset of

```
public class BoundedBufferV1 {
  private Book array[];
  private int takePtr = 0, putPtr = 0;
  protected int usedSlots = 0, size;
  BoundedBufferV1(int capacity) throws IllegalArgumentException {
    if (capacity <= 0) throw new IllegalArgumentException();
    array = new Object[capacity];
    size = capacity ;
  }
  public int count() { return usedSlots; }
  public int capacity() { return size; }
  public void put(Book x) throws Full {
    if (usedSlots == array.length) throw new Full();
    array[putPtr] = x;
    putPtr = (putPtr + 1) % size;
    usedSlots++;
    System.out.println("BB got book:");
    b.print();
  }
  public Book take() throws Empty {
    if (usedSlots == 0) throw new Empty();
    Book old = array[takePtr];
    takePtr = (takePtr + 1) % size;
    usedSlots--;
    return old;
  }
}
public class Book {
  private int isbn = 0;
  private String title = null;
  private Postscript ps;
  Book(int n, String t) {isbn = n; title = t;}
  public void print() {
    System.out.println ("Book: " + isbn + title);
  }
}
```

FIGURE 3.7. BoundedBuffer example (reproduced from Lopes [65]).

methods of the class that can be invoked remotely, and the parameters and return values of those methods. For each parameter and return value the programmer may optionally define the mode that describes how the data transfers are to be made, copy-by-value or copy-by-reference.

For example, given the class[6] in Figure 3.7 the portal:

```
portal BoundedBufferV1 {
  int capacity();
  void put(Book x);
  Book take();
}
```

states that:

- The methods **capacity**, **put** and **take** are remote methods.
- The method **count**, as it has not been defined in the portal, is a local method.
- The **Book** argument to the **put** method and the **Book** return value from the **take** method are passed and returned respectively using the default transfer strategy, copy-by-value.

If, instead, the programmer wishes to use the copy-by-reference semantics, the following portal can be defined using the **gref** (for global reference) keyword:

```
portal BoundedBufferV1 {
  int capacity();
  void put(Book x) {
    x: gref;
  }
  Book take() {
    return: gref;
  }
}
```

However by doing so, the **Book** class must now be defined as a remote object as well:

```
portal Book {
  void print();
}
```

The application that instantiates the bounded buffer class, defined in Figure 3.7, must export a reference to that instance in the name server as illustrated below:

```
public class StartBuffer {
  public static void main(String args[]) {
    BoundedBufferV1 bb = new BoundedBufferV1(100);
    try {
      DJNaming.bind("rmi://goblin/BB", bb);
    } catch (Exception e) {
      System.out.println("StartBuffer err: " + e.getMessage());
      e.printStackTrace();
    }
  }
}
```

---

[6]The examples in this section are reproduced from Lopes [65].

RIDL's DJNaming class is a wrapper class that interacts with Java's RMI Naming class and is therefore tied to a single protocol, RMI. Objects that export these remote object references are explicitly tied to the RIDL specific naming framework, thereby tying them to the framework.

Client calls to remote methods are exactly the same as calls to local methods with the following exceptions:

- The run-time exception DJInvalidRemoteOp may be thrown.
- RIDL framework elements must be used to locate the remote method.

For example, to bind to the remote object, BoundedBuffer, the RIDL specific naming framework must be used:

```
BoundedBuffer1 bb = new BoundedBuffer(100);
String url = "rmi://parc.xerox.com/BoundedBuffer";
// bind url to remote object
DJNaming.bind(url, bb);
   ...
// lookup bounded buffer
bb = (BoundedBuffer)DJNaming.lookup(url);
```

One of the compelling features of RIDL is the ability to pass or return partial copies of objects in the remote call. For example, the portal:

```
portal BoundedBufferV1 {
  int capacity();
  void put(Book x) {
    x: gref;
  }
  Book take() {
    return: copy { Book bypass title, ps; }
  }
}
```

declares that the returned Book object does not contain the title or ps fields. This feature can dramatically reduce the overhead of a remote call. If the programmer inadvertently refers to the title or ps fields, an error is generated.

RIDL programmers are required to adhere to RIDL's naming framework and the use of the RIDL specific exception, DJInvalidRemoteOp. RIDL is therefore not entirely transparent to the programmer and by being so is intrusive in nature although this intrusiveness is fairly limited.

3.8.1.2   AWED

AWED [73] is a comprehensive aspect language for distribution which provides remote pointcuts, distributed advice, and distributed aspects and is implemented by extensions to the JAsCo [106] AOP framework called DJAsCo.

The main characteristics of the AWED model are:

Remote pointcuts which can be used to match events on remote hosts, including remote sequences. Sequences define a list of methods that have been executed in order and may be referred to in pointcuts and advice. Remote pointcuts enable the matching of join points on remote hosts and includes remote calls and remote cflow constructs (matching of nested calls over different machines).

Distributed advice execution. Advice can be executed either synchronously or asynchronously.

Distributed aspects which may be configured using different deployment and instantiation options.

The motivation behind the development of the AWED language is transactional cache replication in the JBoss application server and consequently the language supports the notion of distributed hosts with the keyword host and includes the ability to define groups of hosts.

On the occurrence of a join point, AWED evaluates all pointcuts on all hosts where the corresponding aspects are deployed. Pointcuts may contain conditions about hosts where the join point originated and may also be defined in terms where advice is executed [73].

For example[7] the pointcut:

call(void initCache()) && host("adr1:port")

matches calls to the initCache method on the host with the specified address and the advice may be executed on any host where the aspect is deployed [73].

The AWED language is a fairly low-level language and borrows much of its syntax from AspectJ, including the keywords *pointcut, call, after, around* and *before*. In common with RIDL, the AWED language has no support for either multiple protocols (its current implementation uses the RMI protocol exclusively) or the recovery concern.

3.8.2   AspectJ Implementations

Soares et al. [91] illustrate how the AspectJ language can be used to introduce the distribution concern in the form of the RMI protocol into existing non-distributed applications. Soares et al.'s solution utilises two aspects, a client aspect and a server aspect. For the server aspect, a remote interface is generated for each object that is to be distributed and each object is altered to implement the interface. The client aspect redirects local method calls to the now remote object and alters the local methods to declare that they throw the RemoteException exception. Due to AspectJ's inability to allow changes to the target object in its *proceed* statement, a dedicated redirection advice is used to redirect calls to the remote object from the client object.

---

[7]These examples are reproduced from Navarro et al. [73].

Ceccato and Tonella [18] use a static code analyser and code generator to analyse a non-distributed application and generate AspectJ code to apply the distribution concern using the RMI protocol. All public methods in a class are automatically altered to be remote methods and the various RMI specific conventions are applied. In addition, parameters and return values are declared to be remote objects so that they may be passed by reference, instead of the RMI default pass-by-value, to avoid issues that may occur if the object cannot be serialized. However, as identified by Tilevich and Smaragdakis [111], this approach is extremely inefficient as each method call generates network traffic.

3.8.3 J-Orchestra

J-Orchestra [110, 113] is an automatic partitioning system for Java, which uses bytecode rewriting to apply distribution and claims to be able to partition any Java application and allow any application object to be placed on any machine, regardless of how the application objects interact.

Although J-Orchestra's focus is on the automatic partitioning of Java applications and does not employ a domain-specific aspect language or specifically define aspect-oriented concepts, such as join points or pointcuts, its use of bytecode rewriting is essentially an aspect-oriented approach.

J-Orchestra replaces Java's RMI with NRMI [111], a modified version that implements *call-by-copy-restore* semantics for object types for remote calls. In RMI, copy-by-value is used to pass parameters from the client to the server. That is, parameter objects are serialized and copied to the server. However, any changes to parameter objects on the server are lost when the call returns. Call-by-copy-restore overcomes this by copying changes made on the server back to the client which is, to the user, more natural as it emulates a local procedure call. However, inevitably, additional network traffic is generated.

J-Orchestra implements distributed thread management [112] so that multi-threaded applications can behave in the same manner once they are automatically partitioned. Distributed thread management is implemented by altering only the thread specific bytecode with calls to operations of the J-Orchestra distribution-aware synchronisation library. Again, this has an overhead on network traffic.

Users interact with the J-Orchestra system using XML files, which simply detail a list of classes to be distributed. J-Orchestra has no concept of a domain-specific language, multiple protocols or user-defined definition and manipulation of the recovery concern. Nevertheless it does, for the RMI protocol, provide sophisticated automatic partitioning.

3.8.4 Other Systems

Both JavaParty [83] and DJcutter [74] use a language-based approach and supply Java language extensions to provide explicit support for distribution. Again these systems target the RMI protocol exclusively.

JAC [82] is a dynamic AOP framework that has been extended to support a distributed pointcut definition, which extends the regular pointcut definition with the ability to specify a named host where the join point should be detected. To support the distributed deployment of aspects, JAC replicates its Aspect-Component manager, which is used to keep track of registered aspects on the named hosts. A consistency protocol is used to ensure that the weaving/unweaving of an aspect on one site triggers the weaving or unweaving of the same aspect on other sites [82].

A number of multi-protocol systems, such as RMIX [62] and ACT [29], have been proposed. However, these systems use the high-level framework approach discussed in Section 2.7 and therefore have the same issue as all framework-based approaches, namely tying the application code to the framework or API.

3.8.5 Our Approach

The D language framework concentrated on distributed thread co-ordination and remote access strategies but did not address error handling mechanisms. Indeed Lopes [65], the author of the D language framework, states that error handling was omitted from D, not because it was not a problem, but because it was *too big of a design problem that needed much more research*. Our research addresses this issue by introducing a domain-specific aspect language that provides modularisation not only for the distribution concern but also for the *distribution recovery concern*. In addition we provide support for multiple protocols while other approaches only support a single protocol.

Our approach introduces the concept of a Distribution Definition Language (DDL), a simple high-level domain-specific aspect language, which generalises distributed systems development by describing the classes and methods to be made remote, the protocol to use to make them remote and the method used to recover from a remote error. The DDL is used by the RemoteJ compiler/generator, which uses bytecode manipulation and generation techniques to provide a distributed version of the application while retaining existing classes for reuse in other distributed or non-distributed applications.

By generalising and modularising the distribution and recovery concerns, the use of a DDL provides a method of developing distributed applications that is significantly simplified, allows multiple protocols to be supported for the same code base, allows explicit definition of the recovery concern and enables the same code to be used in both a distributed and non-distributed application thereby improving software reuse.

3.9   Chapter Summary

This chapter has provided the lineage towards the domain-specific aspect language (DSAL) approach to distributed systems development by examining aspect-orientation, aspect-orientation as applied to autonomic systems, aspect-oriented languages and aspect-oriented frameworks and their features and facilities.

Related work in using aspects for distribution, including frameworks, domain-specific languages, Java language extensions and AspectJ approaches, have been discussed.

We have discussed three common implementations of aspect-oriented systems:

1. The language-based approach, which is designed as an extension to an existing language.
2. The object-oriented framework-based approach, which provides a framework that is used by developers to apply aspects to existing code.
3. The domain-specific aspect language approach, which uses a domain-specific language to apply aspects to existing code.

AspectJ [6], an example of the first approach, extends the Java programming language and provides a low level generalised approach to aspect-oriented programming. Because AspectJ, and other language-based systems, are at a low level they are relatively complicated to use. In addition, they introduce additional concepts and constructs, such as the notion of introductions, join points and pointcuts, which further complicates their understanding.

The JBoss AOP [54] framework is an example of the framework-based approach as it allows programmers to define AOP constructs as Java classes using an object-oriented framework. These constructs are used to alter the bytecode of the target application using information contained in an XML file. Object-oriented framework approaches are relatively easy to use compared to the language-based approach as they use the same language as the application. However, this approach requires developers to adhere to the framework's protocol, such as ensuring that `invocation.invokeNext()` is called in an aspect, as is the case with the JBoss AOP framework. Therefore, although framework-based approaches are easier to use than language-based approaches, they require the programmer to have a good understanding of the framework.

KALA [35], a domain-specific aspect language for the transactional domain, is an example of the third approach as it uses a high-level domain-specific aspect language to apply aspects to existing code. Domain-specific aspect languages require the developer to use a different language alongside the application language and therefore require the programmer to learn a new language, although the language is generally relatively simple. Nevertheless domain-specific aspect languages, because they are at a higher level of abstraction, are generally much simpler to use than the other two approaches.

A number of systems and proposals that use AOP to provide autonomics have been discussed. However, none of these approaches are specifically targeted at the distribution concern and therefore do not provide a means of implementing recovery, nor do they generalise the distribution concern. Rather they are either targeted towards a specific domain, such as QoS or NetBSD, or are layered on top of an existing middleware system, which hides the distribution and recovery concerns.

We have introduced our approach consisting of a high-level domain-specific aspect language for the distribution and recovery concerns we call a Distribution Definition Language and the RemoteJ compiler/generator, which is used to apply the distribution and recovery concerns described in the Distribution Definition Language to existing applications. The Distribution Definition Language generalises distributed systems development by describing the classes and methods to be made remote, the protocol to use to make them remote and the method used to recover from a remote error.

The closest work to ours thus far are RIDL and AWED. Both RIDL and AWED use a lower level approach than RemoteJ, which, by introducing the concept of a Distribution Definition Language, is at a higher level of abstraction. In addition, the Distribution Definition Language supports error handling, which is not supported by either RIDL or AWED or indeed any other system to our knowledge.

Autonomics Development: A Domain-Specific Aspect Language Approach, 67–76
Book Series: Autonomic Systems
© 2010 Springer Basel AG

4 The Distribution Definition Language

4.1 Introduction

In Chapter 2 we discussed distributed systems development and the issues surrounding the use of frameworks and programming conventions and the alternative network obliviousness model. Neither of these approaches is satisfactory as they either violate the principle of separation of concerns or attempt to hide distribution and recovery altogether. In the previous chapter we provided an overview of the aspect-oriented paradigm and introduced our approach, the high-level domain-specific aspect language approach, which provides both separation of concerns and network obliviousness without compromising either.

In this chapter we discuss our motivation and the DDL's design principles in Section 4.2 and describe the language grammar in Section 4.3. The formal syntax of the DDL is provided in Appendix A.

4.2 Motivation and Design Principles

In this section we describe our motivation and design principles, which form the basis of our design decisions.

4.2.1 Issues with Distributed Systems Development

Remote Procedure Calls (RPC) were designed to overcome the difficulties of distributed systems development where developers were required to deal with low-level details such as network connections, protocol handling, data representation between different architectures, both partial and 'hard' failures, reassembly of data packets and various other issues. RPCs were designed to behave the same as local procedure calls by masking the difference between local and remote procedure calls so that, to the developer, local and remote procedure calls were essentially equivalent.

However, the developers of RMI argue that the RPC concept of masking the differences between local and remote procedure calls is flawed because there are fundamental differences between the interactions of distributed objects and the interactions of non-distributed objects and attempts to paper over the differences between local and remote objects leads to distributed applications that are neither robust nor reliable [118].

TABLE 4.1. The eight fallacies of distributed computing.

1.	The network is reliable
2.	Latency is zero
3.	Bandwidth is infinite
4.	The network is secure
5.	Topology doesn't change
6.	There is one administrator
7.	Transport cost is zero
8.	The network is homogeneous

This notion is further supported by the infamous 'Eight Fallacies of Distributed Computing' detailed in Table 4.1, which define a set of common but flawed assumptions made by programmers when first developing distributed applications [24].

Consequently the framework provided by RMI requires that the developer be aware of remote objects and remote errors that may occur while interacting with remote objects. This awareness manifests itself in the need for developers to adhere to the RMI specific framework and conventions and to ensure that remote methods throw the RMI specific exception `java.rmi.RemoteException`.

We believe that the developers of RMI are essentially correct in that the programmer needs to be aware of the distributed nature of their application. However, we believe that the *implementation of this requirement* in current Java distributed systems is fundamentally wrong as it leads to code that is polluted with the crosscutting concern *distribution* because the distribution concern crosscuts the application making reuse of application components difficult, if not impossible.

This close coupling between frameworks and application code is not unique to RMI or distribution frameworks, it is inherent in all object-oriented applications that use frameworks. Frameworks may therefore be considered crosscutting in nature because a framework's code is scattered throughout an application's code, either by inheritance or containment, thereby making reuse outside the framework's domain difficult.

4.2.2   Autonomic Computing

As described in Section 4.2.1 above, there are a number of issues with distributed systems development, which are an impediment to the realisation of the vision of autonomic computing. One of our motivations, therefore, is to explore an alternative approach to the development of distributed applications to overcome these impediments.

4.2.3   Separation of Concerns

As discussed in Chapter 2, distributed systems are difficult to write. Programmers need to adhere to specific distributed systems programming conventions and frameworks, which makes distributed systems development complex and error prone and ties the resultant application to the distributed system because the application's code is tangled with the crosscutting concern distribution.

Separation of concerns is a primary design principle [79] yet current distributed systems development techniques require the use of distribution frameworks, programming conventions, or both. Therefore, one of the primary motivations behind our research is to assist developers in modularising the distribution concern and consequently separation of concerns is a primary design principle. However, in contrast with other systems that have similar motivation, such as the D language framework [66] and J-Orchestra [113], we expand the distribution concern into two distinct concerns, distribution implementation and recovery.

While the systems mentioned above assume a single protocol, RMI, we assume multiple protocols, and therefore multiple implementations, and while RIDL and J-Orchestra have no concept of modularising the recovery concern, we consider it a concern in its own right. Although it may be argued that recovery is part of the distribution concern, this is only true if a single protocol is considered. The use of multiple protocols allows the possibility of the same recovery code to be used for multiple protocols and consequently we consider the recovery concern distinct from the distribution concern.

4.2.4   Simplicity

The ultimate goal of the RemoteJ system is to simplify distributed programming as much as possible. In order to achieve this a number of design decisions were made.

- The Distribution Definition Language should be as simple as possible while still allowing sophisticated operations on the underlying program.
- We should not impose a new language on the programmer, rather we should follow the syntax of our target language, Java, as much as possible so that the syntax is intuitive and easy to learn and understand.
- Unless absolutely necessary, aspect-oriented concepts should be hidden from the programmer.
- Features of the various supported distributed systems should be hidden from the programmer as much as possible.

4.3   The Distribution Definition Language

The DDL is a simple language, based on a Java-like syntax, used to describe classes and their methods to be made remote, the protocol to be used, and the action to take in the event of an error. The DDL is designed to support any number of protocols and recovery strategies in the same source file, thereby allowing a single source file to be used to apply distribution to any number of class files.

4.3.1 Comments

Comments in the DDL are the same as for the Java language.

end of line
    Line comments start with '//' and end at the end of the line
multi line
    Multi line comments start with /* and end with */

4.3.2 Keywords

The DDL reserves the following keywords, which therefore cannot be used as identifiers. We discuss these keywords in subsequent sections.

Keyword:
    import | service | recovery | protocol | serverPlugin |
    options | pointcut | nextServer | abort | continue

4.3.3 Import Statements

The `import` statement is used to avoid having to use fully qualified class names when referring to Java classes in the DDL. They are therefore equivalent to the use of Java's `import` statement. The `import` statement is defined as follows:

$$ImportNameList ::= SingleImport\ (SingleImport)*$$
$$SingleImport\quad ::= \mathbf{import}\ Imports\ Semi$$
$$Imports\qquad\quad ::= Identifier\ (Dot\ |\ Wildcard)*$$

The DDL specification/program may contain any number of `import` statements and, in common with Java's convention, `import` statements may only appear at the beginning of the DDL file.

The wildcard character '*' may be used to refer to all classes in a particular Java package.

4.3.4 Service Statement

The `service` statement is used to describe one or more protocols, and associated classes, and one or more `recovery` statements. The name used for the service must be the same as the name of the DDL file with the extension `ddl`, for example the service named `TestService` must be contained in the file `TestService.ddl`. The `service` statement is defined as:

$$Service ::= \mathbf{service}\quad Identifier\ LeftCurley\ StatementList\ RightCurley$$

The service name is used by the compiler/generator as the directory name for generated classes prefixed, by default, by either 'client', for client classes, or 'server' for server classes. For example, a service named `TestService` will have the altered and generated classes placed in the directories `client/TestService` and `server/TestService`. These names may be overridden by stipulating different values on the compiler/generator command line.

4.3.5   Service Recovery Statements

The DDL supports two `recovery` statements, a service recovery statement, which is defined as part of a service and contains the code to be executed in the event of a distribution exception, and a pointcut recovery statement defined as part of a `pointcut` statement, which refers to the service recovery routine to use in the event of a distribution error or one of a number of built-in recovery routines. This section discusses the service recovery statement. Pointcut recovery statements are discussed in Section 4.3.8.

Service `recovery` statements are used to provide the code to be called in the event of distribution exceptions. Any valid Java code may be stipulated, which allows a great deal of control over the recovery mechanism as the programmer is free to provide any recovery implementation not explicitly supported in the language, providing it can be found by the RemoteJ compiler/generator (i.e. in the compiler's `CLASSPATH`). The service recovery statement is defined as:

$$
\begin{aligned}
&\textit{RecoveryList} &&::= \textit{RecoveryStatement (RecoveryStatement)}^* \\
&\textit{RecoveryStatement} &&::= \textbf{recovery}\;\; \textit{RecoveryName LeftBracket ClassName} \\
&&&\quad \textit{Variable RightBracket LeftCurley JavaStatement} \\
&&&\quad \textit{RightCurley} \\
&\textit{JavaStatement} &&::= \textit{Any Java statement accepted by Javassist [19]}
\end{aligned}
$$

Any number of `recovery` statements may be provided but will only be invoked if called by one or more `pointcut` recovery statements.

Recovery statements have access to the context of the remote method call via RemoteJ's internal `Transfer` object. This object contains the remote server name, the class and method that was called, and the method's parameters and return type.

Recovery statements are defined with the keyword **recovery** followed by the name of the recovery statement and the exception to be caught.

In the example in Figure 4.1, `RemoteException` is used as the exception type. Some protocols supported by the RemoteJ DDL may not, however, use `RemoteException` to indicate that an error has occurred. In these cases, the exception type provided by the protocol may be used. In the cases where error codes are used in place of exceptions, the protocol implementation is responsible for providing an exception hierarchy and appropriate mapping between error codes and exceptions.

```
recovery remoteError (RemoteException e) {
    System.out.println("Exception: " + e.getMessage());
    System.out.println("Host : " + transfer.getCurrentHost());
    System.out.println("Failed method call : " + transfer.getMethod());
}
```

FIGURE 4.1. Recovery statement example.

4.3.6   Protocol Statements

The **protocol** statement is used to define the protocol to be used, the protocol options, the classes and associated methods to be altered to use the protocol and the recovery strategy to be used.

$$ProtocolStatement ::= \textbf{protocol } Identifier \; Colon \; LeftCurley$$
$$Options \; (PointcutStatement) + \; RightCurley$$

There may be any number of **protocol** statements and there may be more than one **protocol** statement for the same protocol. Each protocol statement must contain a single option statement and one or more **pointcut** statements.

4.3.7   Options Statements

As can be expected, different protocols may have different protocol options and these options are stipulated in the **options** statement contained in the **protocol** statement.

As there may be more than one protocol in a single application (or perhaps the same protocol with different options, for example), any number of protocol and associated option statements may be declared. Option statements are simple name/value pairs using the following syntax:

$$Options \qquad ::= (Identifier \; = \; Identifier) +$$
$$Identifier \qquad ::= ('a'..'z' \; | \; 'A'..'Z') + (IntegerLiteral) *$$
$$IntegerLiteral \; ::= 0..255$$

Options and protocols are not part of the DDL language as such. Instead, the RemoteJ parser/generator accepts any string for the protocol and any name/value pairs for the options and defers protocol and protocol option checking to plug in *protocol adapters*.

This allows additional protocols to be added without changes needing to be made to the RemoteJ parser. We describe this process in full in Section 5.2.

4.3.8   Pointcut Statements

The **pointcut** statement contains the class and associated methods that are to become distributed using the protocol stipulated in the **protocol** statement. In addition, the recovery strategy may be stipulated for those matched methods. Pointcut statements are described as:

PointcutStatement	::=	**pointcut** *Return Value PointcutName*
		LeftBracket (((Parameter)? (Comma Parameter)*)
		| *Parameter Wildcard)*
		RightBracket LeftCurley RecoveryType RightCurley
Return Value	::=	*ClassName* | *PrimitiveType* | **void**
PointcutName	::=	*Identifier (Dot Identifier* | *Wildcard)**
Parameter	::=	*ClassName* | *PrimitiveType*
RecoveryType	::=	**recovery** *Equals RecoveryOption Semi*
RecoveryOption	::=	*RecoveryName* | **continue** | **abort** | **nextServer**
RecoveryName	::=	*Identifier*
ClassName	::=	*Identifier (Dot Identifier)**
PrimitiveType	::=	**boolean** | **byte** | **char** | **short** | **int** | **long**
		| **float** | **double**
Wildcard	::=	*****
Parameter Wildcard	::=	**..**

The `pointcut` statement supports the use of the asterisk wildcard character. For example, the following statement:

> **pointcut** * Address.* (String, String);

stipulates that all methods in the class **Address** (**Address.***) with two parameters of the type **String** that have any type as a return statement (**'*'**) are selected.

In addition, wildcard parameters are supported. The following statement:

> **pointcut** * Address.* (..);

stipulates that all methods in the class **Address** (**Address.***) with any parameters that have any type as a return statement (**'*'**) are selected.

A compiler error is generated if a method is matched by more than one `pointcut` statement.

The `pointcut recovery` statement may either refer to a user-defined recovery statement, described in Section 4.3.5 or one of three built-in recovery statements that may be used to aid recovery:

nextServer: The protocol implementation should attempt to recover from a remote error by finding an additional server.

abort: The protocol implementation should stop in the event of a remote error.

continue: The protocol implementation should ignore remote errors.

4.4   Influences

The concept of a Distribution Definition Language has been broadly influenced by the Interface Definition Language (IDL) concept. An IDL is a specification language used to describe the interfaces between client and server applications in a language-neutral way and is used by many different distributed systems, such as the Networking Computing Architecture [26], Sun's ONC [98] and CORBA [77] amongst others[1].

In common with an IDL, the DDL allows for the definition of remote interfaces. However, the DDL differs from an IDL in a number of important ways:

- Unlike the DDL, an IDL has no concept of the recovery concern and most implementations use the RPC concept of hiding the application's distributed nature.
- The DDL assumes a single implementation language, Java, while IDLs are generally designed to support multiple languages.
- IDL's generate stubs and skeletons, as described in Section 2.3.6, which are used by the developer to implement the client and server portions of the application. In contrast, the DDL requires the classes and associated methods defined in the DDL to exist so that the compiler may rewrite the bytecode directly.

4.5   Current Limitations

There are a number of limitations in the DDL that restrict the types of distributed applications that the RemoteJ system is suitable for.

4.5.1   Callbacks

There is currently no support for *callbacks*, in the case where a server calls back into a client, or support for a server that is also a client to another server, which may possibly use a different protocol.

While RemoteJ is not unique in this limitation (the limitation is present in both RIDL [65] and J-Orchestra [113]) the class of applications to which RemoteJ may be applied to is limited as a result. For example, applications that implement a server process that needs to inform multiple clients via a callback of a state change cannot currently be supported. This is an area for additional research.

4.5.2   Object Passing

Some protocols, such as RMI, allow objects to be passed either by reference or by value. If the object to be passed is a remote object (it implements the `java.rmi.Remote` interface) a remote reference is passed. If, however, the object is not a remote object, a copy of the object is passed and changes to that copy are not reflected in the client (in the case of parameters) or server (in the case of a

---

[1]See Section 2.3.6 for an overview of Sun's ONC IDL and Section 2.4 for an overview of the CORBA IDL.

returned object). Changes to the object may therefore either be reflected on the client (or server) or not depending on how the object has been defined.

The DDL currently does not support pass-by-reference semantics as supported by RIDL [65] or call-by-copy-restore as supported by J-Orchestra [111]. Instead our implementations implement copy-by-value for all protocols as discussed in Section 5.7. DDL support for pass-by-reference and call-by-copy-restore are an area for further research.

4.5.3 Concurrency

Automatic partitioning systems, such as J-Orchestra [113], attempt to transparently partition applications and so to provide distributed thread management. We believe this approach cannot work in all circumstances, as verified by Tilevich [110], and therefore our approach is to ensure that applications are written with distribution in mind and need to be aware of concurrency issues. This approach is consistent with current Java distribution protocols, which do not support distributed thread co-ordination.

We therefore do not specifically address concurrency and delegate thread management to the programmer.

To assist the programmer with concurrency issues, the RemoteJ compiler/generator will issue an error if a pointcut matches a method defined as **synchronized** or if the method contains **synchronized** blocks of code.

4.6 Chapter Summary

This chapter presented our concept of a Distribution Definition Language, a high-level domain-specific aspect language used to apply the distribution concern to existing Java objects. Our motivation for the DDL was to modularise the distribution and recovery concerns so that separation of concerns can be maintained and distributed systems development can be simplified.

The DDL generalises distributed systems development by describing the classes and methods to be made remote, the distributed system to use to make them remote and the recovery mechanism to use in the event of a remote error. This allows a single component to be reused in multiple distributed applications as well as in other non-distributed applications, thereby improving reuse and simplifying testability of application code.

The DDL's support for distribution error recovery modularises the recovery concern. As well as providing support for common recovery scenarios, the DDL also allows user-defined recovery routines, which greatly enhances its capability.

The above DDL capability allows RemoteJ to support the development of a large proportion of distributed applications in a greatly simplified way compared to the traditional IDL or framework approach.

Autonomics Development: A Domain-Specific Aspect Language Approach, 77–95
Book Series: Autonomic Systems

5 The RemoteJ Compiler/Generator Implementation

5.1 Introduction

In this chapter we describe the implementation of the RemoteJ compiler/generator. We describe the compiler and its features and discuss the implementation of the recovery concern and the JMS, REST and RMI protocol implementations.

5.2 Compiler/Generator Overview

The RemoteJ compiler is a simple three-phase compiler/generator, illustrated in Figure 5.1, that is used to apply distribution to existing bytecode using instructions contained in a Distribution Definition Language file.

The compiler/generator consists of three phases; syntactic analysis phase, the contextual analysis phase and the code rewriting phase.

The syntactic analysis phase checks the syntax of the DDL file and generates an abstract syntax tree (AST) representation. The AST is passed into the contextual analysis phase, which ensures that the context of the grammar conforms to the DDLs contextual constraints and decorates the AST with information about the parameters, scope rules, types etc. The decorated AST is passed into the aspect weaver, which rewrites the existing bytecode and outputs the resultant file into the location stipulated by the DDL's `service` statement as described in Section 4.3.4.

The RemoteJ compiler/generator has been developed to the compiler/interpreter patterns defined by Watt and Brown [119].

The compiler/generator supports any number of back-end code generators using an extendible dynamic model that eliminates the need for changes to be made to the compiler/generator for the addition of new protocols or protocol options.

A high-level view of the extendible code generation support is illustrated in Figure 5.2.

To add a new protocol, the developer extends the `Protocol` class, which implements the `IProtocol` interface, illustrated in Figure 5.3. The `Protocol` class contains generalised aspect-weaving code, such as generating recovery routines and altering a class to implement an interface, and other useful routines including

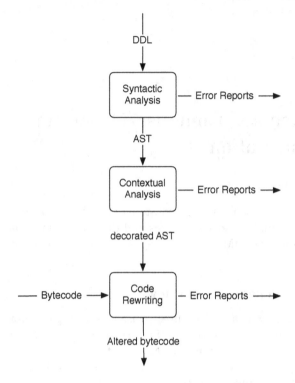

FIGURE 5.1. Compiler data flow.

methods to check if a class implements the serializable interface, renaming class files and checking a method's return type.

At runtime, the name of the protocol is used to dynamically load the protocol implementation class and defer code generation and protocol option checking functionality to it using the following mechanism:

- The name of the protocol contained in the DDL is converted to upper case.
- The package name org.remotej.generated. is prefixed to the protocol name.
- The word Protocol is appended to the above.
- The class is dynamically loaded and instantiated using Java's Class class.

Using the above mechanism, a protocol with the name jms will be converted to org.remotej.generated.JMSProtocol and will be loaded and instantiated by the ProtocolFactory class using the Class.forName(className).newInstance() mechanism provided by Java's Class class. Protocol options are collected by the compiler's parser and are passed to the protocol implementation for verification and subsequent use in the code generation phase.

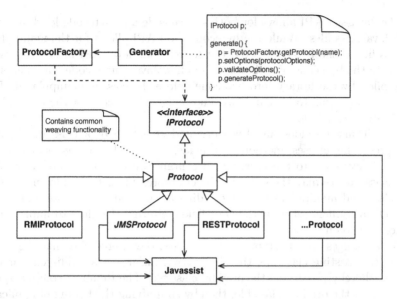

FIGURE 5.2. Extendible code generation support.

```java
public interface IProtocol {
    void validateOptions() throws OptionException;
    void setOptions(ProtocolOptions opt);
    void setServerOutputDirectory(String serverOutputDirectory);
    void setClientOutputDirectory(String clientOutputDirectory);
    void setService(String spelling);
    void setImports(Vector<String> imports);
    void setReporter(ErrorHandler reporter);
    void setLineNumber(SourcePosition position);
    void setRecovery(Vector<JavaMethod> recovery);
    void setProtocolDescription(ProtocolDescription protocols);
    void generateAll();
}
```

FIGURE 5.3. IProtocol class.

This approach makes it relatively easy to add additional protocols as no changes need to be made to the language or the compiler/generator to support new protocols and their options.

5.2.1   Bytecode Rewriting

The RemoteJ compiler/generator uses the Javassist [19] library, a bytecode rewriting library used by the JBoss AOP framework [54], for all bytecode rewriting.

The Javassist API allows for both source code and bytecode level manipulation of Java class files. While the bytecode level API allows for the manipulation of a class file at the bytecode level, the source code level API allows the user to manipulate the bytecode of a class by providing Java source code statements that are compiled by the library into bytecode before the class is manipulated. Users therefore do not need to have detailed knowledge of bytecode or the internal Java class file structures [19].

The library provides an object-oriented structure of a class file with objects representing classes, methods and fields. Once a class file is loaded, a class, CtClass, is available to the user, which contains an object-oriented view of the loaded class. Users may then obtain objects representing the fields and methods of the class and manipulate them by adding advice code before, around or after a method, introducing new methods or fields, altering the class to implement an interface and so on.

Once changes have been made to the class, the altered class may be written to either the existing class file, thereby overwriting it, or to a different directory structure, thereby preserving the original class file. The RemoteJ compiler/generator preserves the original class file, thereby simplifying the testing of application code, as the system may be tested as a non-distributed application, using testing tools such as JUnit [11] and run as a distributed application using any supported protocol.

The RemoteJ compiler/generator uses the source code level API for all bytecode manipulation with the exception of identifying synchronized blocks of code, which uses the bytecode level API.

5.3   Recovery Implementation

The RemoteJ DDL supports four recovery scenarios:

- A user-defined recovery statement that may consist of any valid Java code. In addition, the programmer has access to the Transfer object, illustrated in Figure 5.5, which provides access to the current system state. We also provide access to various helper methods that allows the user to explicitly define a list of available hosts or a particular alternate host to switch to in the event of an error. In addition, we provide the serverPlugin statement, which may be used to provide advanced recovery scenarios, which is described below[1].
- The abort statement, which simply causes the application to terminate.
- The continue statement, which causes the application to ignore the error and continue execution.
- The nextServer statement, which causes the client to switch to the next available server.

---

[1]A recovery implementation illustrating the usage of this statement is provided in Section 6.4.2.

```
public void foo(String name) throws java.rmi.RemoteException {
    boolean done = false;
    do {
      try {
        IFooFoo stub = (IFooFoo)getRegistry().lookup("registry");
        stub.foo(name);
        return;
      } catch (java.rmi.RemoteException e) {
        findAlternateServer();
      }
    } while (!done);
    return;
}
```

FIGURE 5.4. RMI client generated method.

To implement the recovery scenarios, we use helper classes in the client protocol implementation, which consists of generic recovery code. The code in the helper class is merged with the client classes (the classes matched in the DDL statements) and each matching method referred to in the DDL is wrapped with code that calls the remote implementation and, in the event of an error, the user-defined recovery routine. For example, for the RMI implementation, the call to a remote method called foo(String name) with the nextServer recovery method defined in the DDL, results in the code in Figure 5.4 being generated:

In the case where a recovery statement has been defined in the DDL, the findAlternateServer() method call in Figure 5.4 is replaced by the user-defined code. If the abort or continue statement has been defined, then findAlternateServer() is replaced with System.exit(1); and done = true; respectively.

The implementation of the DDL recovery routine nextServer cycles through a list of comma-separated host names or IP addresses that have either been defined in the DDL or in the system property, remotej.servers. If the system property remotej.servers has been defined it overrides values specified in the DDL. To guard against a continuous loop, if all hosts have been tried in sequence and communication to all hosts is unsuccessful, the application will be terminated as we consider this an unrecoverable error.

For user-defined recovery routines, in addition to the Transfer object we provide access to three methods, getCurrentHost(), findAlternateServer() (the same method used by the nextServer DDL statement implementation) and setHosts(String[] hosts) that can be used to aid the programmer in binding to an alternate server. This, used in conjunction with programmer-provided classes that may be used alongside generated classes, allows for highly configurable user-defined recovery scenarios.

For example, the recovery routine:

```
recovery Error (RemoteException e) {
    String[] s = new String[2];
    s[0] = "host1";
    s[1] = "host2";
    setHosts(s);
}
```

resets the list of hosts to host1 and host2. For user-defined recovery routines, RemoteJ generates code to ensure that if calls to both host1 and host2 fail in sequence, the system will not enter an infinite loop by continuously calling the recovery routine. In this instance we assume recovery is impossible and we terminate the application.

An alternative user-defined implementation may be to obtain the list of available hosts from a user-defined routine such as the example below.

```
recovery Error (RemoteException e) {
    String[] s = MyRecovery.getAvailableHosts();
    setHosts(s);
}
```

In this case, the user-defined routine, MyRecovery, must be made available at both compile time and runtime and the package name must be stipulated in the DDL's import statement.

The Transfer object, illustrated in Figure 5.5, contains the system's current state, which is generated and inserted by the RemoteJ compiler/generator at the point when a remote method is about to be called. This contains the method to be called, the method's parameters, the return object and the host that will be called. As well as being available to user-defined recovery routines, the Transfer object is also used for some protocol implementations. This is described in detail in Section 5.5.2.

User-defined recovery routines have the ability to interact with generated server code by the use of server plugins. Server plugin classes are classes that extend Java's Thread class and are stipulated in the protocol's serverPlugin option. The RemoteJ compiler/generator will instantiate the user-defined server plugin at server startup and the plugin will be run in the server process in a separate thread.

This option is intended to allow for the development of user-defined code to interact with user-defined client-side recovery routines. For example, a server plugin may announce its presence on the network in the event it receives a request to do so. In the event of a failure, the user-defined recovery routine may switch to an alternate server by broadcasting a message on the network and choosing the first responding server. We evaluate this functionality in full in Section 6.4.2.

```java
public class Transfer implements Serializable {
    private String className;
    private String method;
    private Object[] parameters;
    private Class[] parameterTypes;
    private Object returnValue;
    private String currentHost;

    public String getCurrentHost() {
        return currentHost;
    }
    public void setCurrentHost(String currentHost) {
        this.currentHost = currentHost;
    }
    public Class[] getParameterTypes() {
        return parameterTypes;
    }
    public void setParameterTypes(Class[] parameterTypes) {
        this.parameterTypes = parameterTypes;
    }
    public String getClassName() {
        return className;
    }
    public void setClassName(String className) {
        this.className = className;
    }
    public String getMethod() {
        return method;
    }
    public void setMethod(String method) {
        this.method = method;
    }
    public Object[] getParameters() {
        return parameters;
    }
    public void setParameters(Object[] parameters) {
        this.parameters = parameters;
    }
    public Object getReturnValue() {
        return returnValue;
    }
    public void setReturnValue(Object returnValue) {
        this.returnValue = returnValue;
    }
}
```

FIGURE 5.5. Recovery Transfer object.

5.4   RMI Protocol Implementation

RMI is a Java-centric distributed system that is used as the protocol for Enterprise JavaBeans (EJB) [103], Jini [117] and JavaSpaces [40]. The RMI framework is very intrusive in nature, as it requires developers to be aware of remote objects and remote errors that may occur while interacting with remote objects. This intrusiveness manifests itself in the need for RMI applications to follow both a programming convention and a programming framework.

The RMI programming conventions are as follows:

- The methods that are to be made available to remote clients must be declared in an interface that extends `java.rmi.Remote`.
- These methods must be declared to throw the `java.rmi.RemoteException` exception.
- RMI uses Java's object serialization to marshal and unmarshal parameters and return values, which encodes objects and any objects they refer to, into a byte stream for transmission from one virtual machine to another. Once the byte stream is received, it is converted into the original object using a process known as deserialization. RMI therefore requires that all objects and any objects they reference that are used as parameters or return values implement the `java.io.Serializable` interface, a marker interface that indicates to the serialization system that they may be safely converted to a byte stream.

In addition, the developer is required to use RMI framework classes to:

- Access the RMI registry.
- Bind an object to the registry.
- Remove an object from the registry.
- Find an object in the registry.
- Export an object either implicitly, by extending the `java.rmi.server.UnicastRemoteObject` class, or explicitly by exporting the object using the `exportObject` method of the same class.

5.4.1   RMI Protocol Implementation Overview

Our RMI implementation is contained in a single class, `RMIProtocol`, which extends from the abstract `Protocol` class, described in Section 5.2. The RMI implementation supports the following options defined in the options DDL statement:

registryName. Defines the name of the remote service that is bound in the RMI registry. It is used by the generated server as the name of the remote service and by clients to locate the remote service.

registryHost. Defines the name of the host where the service is to be run. This option is used by clients, together with the `registryName` option above and the `registryPort` option below, to locate and bind to the remote service. It may be overridden by defining an alternate host, or a list of hosts containing the same service, on the command line or in the recovery statement

TABLE 5.1. RMI generated output files.

Type	Name	Purpose
Client Files	ClockService.class	The client class file that connects to the remote service getDate() contained in the generated ClockDate server class
	_IClockDate.class	The RemoteJ generated RMI interface class
Server Files	ClockDate.class	The server class file that contains the remote service getDate()
	RMIServer.class	The RemoteJ generated RMI server class

using the setHosts() method. If a list of hosts is defined, it is used by the recovery routine to bind to an alternate server if the current server becomes unavailable.

registryPort. Defines the RMI registry port number used by clients to bind to a server. If the runEmbeddedRegistry option described below is defined, it is used as the port number for the embedded registry.

runEmbeddedRegistry. If defined, an embedded RMI registry is started. If not, the registry defined by the registryHost and registryPort options must be available at runtime for the generated server to export the remote objects to, and for the generated client to bind to, so that it may locate the exported objects.

serverPlugin. This optional statement is used to add a user-defined class to be started in a thread in the server-generated code. It is provided to allow for advanced user-defined recovery scenarios as described in Section 5.3.

servers. This optional statement is used to define a comma-separated list of servers that clients may connect to. If defined, it is used by the nextServer statement to connect to an alternate server in the event of a communication or distribution error. This may be overridden by the remotej.servers command line option. If neither servers nor remotej.servers have been defined, the application will terminate.

Given a DDL with the single pointcut statement illustrated in Figure 5.6, the classes in Table 5.1 are generated.

The RMI implementation has the following code generation phases:

Interface generation phase. Used to generate interfaces that extend the java.rmi.Remote interface and contain all matching methods referred to in the DDL. If more than one class is matched by a pointcut in the DDL, multiple interfaces are generated, one for each class containing the matched methods of that class.

Server generation phase. Matching classes and associated methods defined in the DDL are altered to implement the interface described above.

```
import java.rmi.*;
import clock.*;

service ClockService {

  recovery Error (RemoteException e) {
    System.out.println("Method: " + transfer.getMethod());
        System.out.println("Host : " + transfer.getCurrentHost());
        String[] s = new String[2];
        s[0] = "hosts1";
        s[1] = "hosts2";
        setHosts(s);
        System.out.println("Switching to alternate hosts");
  }

  protocol : rmi {
    options {
          registryName = "RMITestServer";
          registryHost = "localhost";
          registryPort = 1099;
          runEmbeddedRegistry = true;
        }
        pointcut Date ClockDate.getDate () {
          recovery = Error;
        }
  }
}
```

FIGURE 5.6. RMI ClockService DDL.

Client generation phase. Matching classes and associated methods defined in the DDL are altered to call an RMI server.

Server bootstrap. A simple RMI server main class is generated and matching classes and methods referred to in the DDL are exported as RMI remote objects. Optionally, an RMI Registry is created to hold references to the exported objects.

Each phase of the implementation is described in detail below.

5.4.2   RMI Interface Generation Phase

In order to generate the interfaces, a list of classes that match the classes referred to in the DDL is generated. For example the DDL statement:

pointcut * Address.* (String, String)

results in a list of all public methods defined in the **Address** class having any return type and two parameters of type **String**. Once a list of matching methods has been collected, they are evaluated to ensure they adhere to the RMI-

specific requirement of having their parameters and return values implement the
java.io.Serializable interface.

Using the list of classes and associated matched methods, one or more interfaces that extend the java.rmi.Remote interface are generated. Each method
that is added to the interface is declared to throw the java.rmi.RemoteException
exception.

5.4.3 RMI Server Generation Phase

Each matching method defined by pointcut statements is checked to ensure they
are defined as public, non-transient and non-native. If any of these checks fail, a
compiler error is generated or, if the checks are successful, the class is altered to
implement the generated interface described in Section 5.4.2.

The altered class file is written to the server sub-directory located under the
directory defined by the DDL Service statement described in Section 4.3.4.

5.4.4 RMI Client Generation Phase

In the client generation phase a number of methods and fields, used to implement the recovery concern described in Section 5.3, are added to each client class
matched by pointcuts declared in the DDL.

As discussed in Section 4.5.3, distributed thread management is not supported so each matched method is checked to ensure that it does not contain the
synchronized keyword and there are no synchronized blocks in the methods. If
so, an error is generated. The existing method call is then replaced with an RMI
client version. E.g., the method:

```
public void foo(String name) {
    // implementation code
}
```

contained in the class FooFoo with a recovery option of nextServer will be replaced with the code in Figure 5.4.

The altered class file is written to the client sub-directory located under the
directory defined by the DDL Service statement described in Section 4.3.4.

5.4.5 RMI Server Bootstrap

To bootstrap the server a class, org.remotej.RMIServer, is generated with a
main method defined that uses the RMI framework to:

1. Set the Java security manager to the RMISecurityManager.
2. Either locate an existing registry or start an embedded one.
3. For each class containing remote methods, the class is exported using the
   UnicastRemoteObject.exportObject() method and the returned stub is
   retrieved.
4. Finally, the returned stubs obtained from the call described above is added
   to the RMI registry.

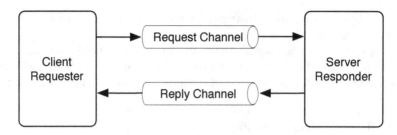

FIGURE 5.7. JMS request/reply pattern.

5.5 JMS Protocol Implementation

The Java Messaging System (JMS) [47] is a Java API for accessing Message-Oriented Middleware (MOM) systems. JMS is supported by most enterprise messaging vendors and, as JMS is part of the Java Enterprise Edition (JEE) specification, it is supported by all JEE vendors. JMS is an asynchronous protocol that provides both Topics, for publish/subscribe type interactions, and Queues, for point-to-point interactions.

Our implementation supports point-to-point interactions using the JMS request/reply pattern [50], illustrated in Figure 5.7, which sends a request message to a server via a send queue and awaits a response on a receive queue.

5.5.1 JMS Protocol Implementation Overview

To simplify implementation and to provide a multithread container that can support multiple simultaneous client requests, we use the following JMS features from the Spring Framework [53] in our implementation:

- The JmsTemplate class for JMS client (message sending and receiving) features.
- The SessionAwareMessageListener, which provides a multithreaded JMS messaging container.

The JMS implementation is contained in a single class, JMSProtocol, which extends from the abstract Protocol class and supports the following options:

initialContextFactory. The JMS JNDI [100] context that is used to obtain access to the JMS implementation.

persist. If defined and set to 'true', persistent messages are used for both receiving and sending.

sendQueue. The name of the queue used to send messages.

receiveQueue. The name of the queue to receive message responses. If the name is defined as the special name, temporary, a temporary queue is created.

servers. A comma-separated list defining the address of one or more JMS message brokers in the format required by the underlying JMS implementation (usually a URL). In common with the RMI protocol, if defined it is

TABLE 5.2. JMS generated output files.

Type	Name	Purpose
Client Files	ClockDate.class	The client class file that connects to the remote service getDate() accessed via the generated JMSServer class
	JMSClient.class	The RemoteJ generated JMS client helper class
Server Files	JMSServer.class	The server class file that delegates remote calls to the ClockDate.getDate() method

used by the nextServer statement to connect to an alternative server in the event of a communication or distribution error. This may be overridden by the remotej.servers command line option. If neither servers nor remotej.servers have been defined, the application will terminate.

serverThreads. The number of server threads to create in the JMS container.

receiveTimeout. The period to wait for a message response. In addition, the JMS time-to-live field is set to the receiveTimeout value to ensure stale messages are removed from the queue (if supported by the JMS implementation).

serverPlugin. This optional statement is used to add a user-defined class to be started in a thread in the server-generated code. It is provided to allow for advanced user-defined recovery scenarios as described in Section 5.3.

Given a DDL with the single pointcut statement illustrated in Figure 5.8 the classes in Table 5.2 are generated.

In contrast to the complexity of the RMI implementation, the JMS implementation contains only two code generation phases, the client and the server generation phases.

5.5.2   JMS Client Generation

The JMS client generation phase performs the same checks as described for the RMI implementation to ensure that methods matched by statements defined in the DDL are not defined as synchronized or contain synchronized blocks of code. Client methods matched in the DDL are replaced with method calls that:

- Create an instance of the Transfer object, described in Section 5.3.
- Call various Transfer object methods to set the name of the class and the associated method to be executed, the method's parameter names, and the method's parameter values.
- Use the RemoteJ JMSClient helper class to transmit the Transfer object from the client to the server using the JMS ObjectMessage message type.

On the server, the values contained in the Transfer object are used to call the requested method using the following process.

```
import javax.jms.*;
import clock.*;

service ClockService {

    recovery JMSError (JMSException e) {
        System.out.println("Method: " + transfer.getMethod());
        System.out.println("Host : " + transfer.getCurrentHost());
        String[] s = new String[2];
        s[0] = "tcp://host1:61616";
        s[1] = "tcp://host2:61616";
        setHosts(s);
        System.out.println("Switching to host1 and host2");
    }

    protocol : jms {
    options {
        destinationClass = "org.apache.activemq.command.ActiveMQQueue";
        initialContextFactory
            = "org.apache.activemq.jndi.ActiveMQInitialContextFactory";
        persist = true;
        sendQueue = "REMOTEJ.SEND";
        receiveQueue = "temporary"; // or name e.g. REMOTEJ.RECEIVE
        brokerURL = "tcp://localhost:61616";
        serverThreads = 5;
        receiveTimeout = 5000;
    }

    pointcut Date ClockDate.getDate () {
        recovery = JMSError;
    }
  }
}
```

FIGURE 5.8. JMS ClockService DDL.

The **Transfer** object is extracted from the message and the class name, the method name to call and the method's parameters are extracted from the **Transfer** object. An object cache is then searched for an instance of the requested class using the class name as the key. If an instance exists in the cache it is used for the call, otherwise a new instance is created, put in the cache and used for all subsequent calls. The Java reflection API is then used to make the call using the object instance, the method name and the parameters.

Following the call, the **Transfer** object is set with the result value of the method call and passed back to the client, which extracts the return value and passes it to the caller.

5.5.3   JMS Server Generation

The JMS server generation phase performs the same checks as the RMI server phase to ensure methods matched by pointcuts are defined as public, non-transient and non-native.

The RemoteJ `JMSServer` class implements the Spring Framework's `SessionAwareMessageListener` interface and provides a skeleton JMS container that we use as the basis for the JMS server implementation. The `SessionAwareMessageListener` interface contains a single method, `onMessage()`, which is called by the Spring framework's JMS container upon receipt of a JMS message.

The JMSServer `onMessage()` implementation contains a generic method to read the message, extract the `Transfer` object from the message, create an instance of the class defined in the `Transfer` object, call the method defined in the `Transfer` object after setting its parameter values and set the return value to the return value from the call. Following the method call, the `Transfer` object is sent back to the client using the Spring framework's `JmsTemplate` class.

In the JMS server generation phase a main method is added to the `JMSServer` class, which creates an instance of the `JMSServer` class, creates an instance of the Spring framework's `DefaultMessageListenerContainer` class, configures the `DefaultMessageListenerContainer` instance using values contained in the DDL and calls its `setMessageListener()` method with the instance of the `JMSServer` class as a parameter. The `DefaultMessageListenerContainer` is then started, which allows the `onMessage()` method of the `JMSServer` class instance to be called when messages arrive.

In common with the RMI server implementation, the altered `JMSServer` class file is written to the server sub-directory located under the directory defined by the DDL Service statement described in Section 4.3.4.

5.6   REST Protocol Implementation

Representational State Transfer (REST) is not a protocol as such but an architectural style based on an idealised model of the interactions within a web application and is the foundation for the modern web architecture. REST is intended to invoke an image of how a well-designed web application behaves where a network of web pages forms a network of virtual state machines and a user progresses through an application by selecting a link or submitting a form with each action resulting in a transition to the next state of an application by transferring a representation of that state to the user. The web is the largest example of the REST architecture [39].

In the REST style, software components are recast as network services and clients request resources from servers using the resource's name and location specified as a Uniform Resource Locator (URL) [13]. All interaction is synchronous in nature and uses the HTTP [37] protocol. Requests can also be relayed via a series of proxies, filters and caches [57].

Fielding [38] defines six core design principles for the REST architecture:

- The key abstraction of information is a resource. Resources are named by a URL and any information that can be named can be a resource, e. g. a person, a service, a document etc.
- Resources are represented by bytes and associated metadata to describe those bytes. Access to the concrete representation of data is therefore via a layer of indirection.
- All interactions are context free. Each interaction contains all the information necessary to understand the request.
- A small number of primitive operations are available. These are essentially the HTTP POST, PUT, GET and DELETE operations.
- Operations should be idempotent and representational metadata should be provided to support caching.
- Intermediaries are promoted so that requests may be filtered, redirected, restricted or modified transparently to both the client and the origin server.

Using the REST web service style, one constructs a URL to represent the particular service (or *resource*) offered. For example the URL:

    http://www.glam.ac.uk/students

refers to all students at the University of Glamorgan and the URL:

    http://www.glam.ac.uk/students/computerscience

refers to all students in the computer science department at Glamorgan while the URL:

    http://www.glam.ac.uk/students/psoule

refers to a particular student. Clients access the required student resource using the URL and a representation of the resource is returned. This representation places the client in a state, and when another resource is accessed the new representation that is returned causes the client to be placed in another state. Therefore each resource representation causes the client to change (transfer) state hence the name Representational State Transfer.

Due to its simplicity, REST has become increasingly popular as an alternative form of web services to the SOAP model [42].

5.6.1   REST Protocol Implementation Overview

To implement our REST protocol we use the Restlet framework [2], a simple lightweight REST framework that is suitable for both client-side and server-side web applications.

The REST implementation is contained in a single class, RESTProtocol, which extends from the abstract Protocol class and supports the following options:

TABLE 5.3. REST generated output files.

Type	Name	Purpose
Client Files	Calendar.class	The client class file that has been altered to connect to the remote service contained in the generated RESTServer class
	RESTClient.class	The RemoteJ REST helper client class
Server Files	RESTServer.class	The server class file that hosts the HTTP server provided by the Restlet REST framework
	RemoteJResource.class	The resource class called by the Reslet REST implementation. This class receives client requests and calls the requested method

servers. A comma-separated list defining the address of one or more REST servers in URL format. In common with the JMS and RMI protocols, if defined it is used by the `nextServer` statement to connect to an alternative server in the event of a communication or distribution error. This may also be overridden by the `remotej.servers` command line option.

serverThreads. The number of server threads created by the Restlet HTTP server.

serverPort. The TCP/IP port number to use for the generated HTTP server.

serverPlugin. In common with the other protocols, this optional statement is used to add a user-defined class to be started in a thread in the server-generated code.

Given a DDL with the five pointcut statements illustrated in Figure 5.9, the classes in Table 5.3 are generated.

In common with the JMS implementation, the REST implementation contains two code generation phases, the client and the server generation phases. These phases work identically to, and reuse much of the functionality of, the JMS implementation and therefore won't be discussed further.

5.7 Implementation Issues

As discussed in Section 4.5, the DDL currently does not support pass-by-reference semantics as supported by RIDL [65] or call-by-copy-restore as supported by J-Orchestra [111]. Instead our implementations implement copy-by-value for all protocols as neither the REST nor JMS protocols provide pass-by-reference. Indeed, both the REST and JMS protocols use a simple generalised communication

```
import evaluation.calendar.*;

service CalendarService {
  protocol : rest {
    options {
        servers = "http://localhost";
        serverPort = 61616;
        serverThreads = 5;
    }
    pointcut Appointment[] Calendar.getAppointments(User) {recovery = nextServer;}
    pointcut void Calendar.addAppointment(User, Appointment) {recovery = nextServer;}
    pointcut void Calendar.deleteAppointment(User, Appointment) {recovery = nextServer;}
  }
}
```

FIGURE 5.9. REST CalandarService DDL.

style that does not explicitly support copy-by-value, copy-by-value-restore or pass-by-reference as neither of them are object based.

Our implementations of the REST and JMS request-reply protocols mimic RMI's pass-by-value by the use of object serialisation and we therefore pass both parameter and return values as serialized objects. The limitation of this approach is that all parameters and return values must be serializable and implement the Serializable interface. If not, a compile error is returned. Although the RMI protocol supports pass-by-reference, we do not currently support it. As discussed in Section 4.5 this is an area for further research and we discuss this further in Section 7.3.

5.8   Chapter Summary

In this chapter we have described the implementation of the RemoteJ compiler/ generator and its features and have discussed the implementation of the recovery concern and our three protocol implementations, JMS, REST and RMI.

The recovery implementation allows a great deal of flexibility with common recovery techniques supported by DDL statements and the ability to add user-defined recovery routines.

The RMI, REST and JMS protocols were chosen as they use different approaches to distribution. RMI and REST are synchronous protocols with an intrusive framework and, in the case of RMI, requires the developer to adhere to a programming convention. JMS is an asynchronous protocol implemented as an abstract framework with numerous concrete implementations that may, nevertheless, be used in a synchronous manner. In addition, JMS provides guaranteed message delivery through the use of persistent messages, while RMI and REST do not.

Despite these differences, all protocols were relatively easily implemented using the DDL concept and a great deal of reuse was possible using the abstract `Protocol` class.

Autonomics Development: A Domain-Specific Aspect Language Approach, 97–115
Book Series: Autonomic Systems
© 2010 Springer Basel AG

6 Evaluation

6.1 Introduction

RemoteJ has been designed as an alternative method of developing distributed applications to both the Java RMI convention, which requires developers to be aware of the distributed nature of their applications, and the RPC convention, which attempts to make remote procedure calls transparent to the developer.

Both of the above approaches result in applications tangled with the cross-cutting concern distribution. Previous work, described in Section 3.8, has shown that an aspect-oriented approach can significantly reduce the tangling between application functionality and the distribution concern, thereby making programs easier to write and understand. However, this previous work has assumed a single protocol and has not considered the recovery concern thereby attempting, once again, to mask the difference between local and remote method calls.

We agree with Waldo et al. [118] that any attempt to paper over the differences between local and remote systems is fundamentally wrong, because distributed systems require that the programmer be aware of issues such as latency and partial failures to be able to support basic requirements of robustness and reliability.

This project has extended previous work by considering multiple protocols and the recovery concern and has introduced the concept of a Distribution Definition Language used to define classes and associated methods to be made distributed, the distributed system to use to make them distributed, and the recovery mechanism to use in the event of an error. In this book we have made the following claims about our approach:

- A significantly simplified approach to the development of distributed systems as it allows the same application to be used distributed or not, thereby improving software reusability and simplifying testability of distributed applications.
- The ability to apply distribution and recovery awareness to existing applications in such a way that the application is oblivious of the distribution and recovery mechanism.
- The Distribution Definition Language can easily be extended to support additional protocols by the implementation of protocol plugins without changes needing to be made to the RemoteJ parser.

In this chapter we validate these claims by:

- Evaluating protocol extendibility by providing a case study of the addition of a publish/subscribe event-driven protocol to RemoteJ.
- Comparing the development of a number of simple distributed applications, developed using the RMI, REST and JMS protocols, with the RemoteJ approach. We compare this in terms of reusability, testability and lines of code.
- Evaluating RemoteJ's recovery approach in terms of extendibility, flexibility and the ability to add the recovery concern to existing applications.

6.2   Adding a Protocol – a Case Study

All three of RemoteJ's protocols described thus far use the request/response synchronous model where a message is sent and the system suspends awaiting a response, a model that is used by most RPC type distributed systems. While this may be adequate and suitable for many scenarios, there is a class of application that is more suited to the asynchronous event-driven model, as described in Section 2.6.1.

To fully evaluate RemoteJ and to support our claim that the DDL can easily be extended to support additional protocols by the implementation of protocol plugins without changes needing to be made to the RemoteJ parser, we extended RemoteJ by adding an asynchronous event-driven protocol based on the JMS publish/subscribe model.

An additional motivation for the choice of an asynchronous event-driven protocol was to evaluate if the DDL concept could support both the synchronous and asynchronous models.

6.2.1   The Event-Driven Model

As described in Section 2.6.2, publish/subscribe systems provide a loosely-coupled interaction style where publishers publish events and subscribers subscribe to those events and are subsequently asynchronously notified when an event occurs. Publish/subscribe systems therefore implement a loosely-coupled *event-driven* style of communication [78].

For our evaluation we implemented an event-driven system based on JMS topics as the JMS API [47] provides an asynchronous event-driven topic abstraction.

In contrast to the request/response synchronous model as exemplified by our RMI, REST and JMS implementations, our event-driven implementation defines two protocols, pub for the publish protocol and sub for the subscriber protocol. The reason for this is that publish/subscribe systems are asynchronous and loosely-coupled and therefore there is no notion of a client and a server as there is for RPC type systems. Rather publishers and subscribers are distinct entities that

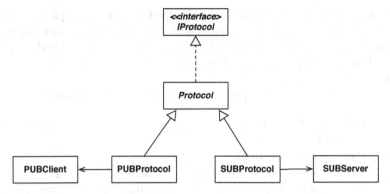

FIGURE 6.1.   Publish/subscribe class diagram. A UML class diagram showing the interaction between the protocol implementation classes.

are decoupled in *time, space* and *synchronisation* [34]. We therefore allow the **pub** and **sub** protocols to be applied to classes independently.

As we do not support multiple methods receiving a single event and multiple methods publishing objects to the same topic, **pointcut** statements must match a single class/method. In addition, for both protocols, the methods matched by the **pointcut** statement in the DDL must meet the following criteria:

- They must have a single serializable parameter that is either sent to the subscriber or received from the producer.
- They must be declared as returning **void**.

Given the above, the method matched by the **pointcut** statement for the **pub** protocol is altered to have its parameter published using options defined for the protocol. The method should contain no code as the parameter is published to the topic and any code in the method will be ignored.

For the **sub** protocol, the matched method receives a published object asynchronously using options defined for the protocol, and the object may be published by any publisher, providing the publishing system is sending serialized Java objects that the **sub** protocol is expecting.

6.2.2   Adding the Protocols

As described in Section 5.2, additional protocols may be added by extending the **Protocol** class, which implements the **IProtocol** interface. The name of the protocol implementation class must be the same as the protocol name in uppercase with the word 'Protocol' appended to it so that it may be dynamically loaded by the **ProtocolFactory** class.

Our two protocols are therefore named **PUBProtocol**, for the **pub** protocol, and **SUBProtocol** for the **sub** protocol. In addition, we developed two helper classes, PUBClient and SUBServer for use by the two protocol implementations respectively. A class diagram for our implementation is illustrated in Figure 6.1. As described in Section 5.2, the Protocol class contains generalised code generation and aspect-weaving capabilities making the addition of new protocols reasonably straight forward.

Both the pub and the sub protocol support the following options:

initialContextFactory. The JMS JNDI [100] context that is used to obtain access to the JMS implementation.

topic. The name of the JMS topic.

servers. A comma-separated list defining the address of one or more JMS message brokers in the format required by the underlying JMS implementation (usually a URL).

In addition, the sub protocol provides the following options to support durable topics as described in Section 2.6.3:

durable. Set to true or false, this declares that durable topics will be used.

subscriber. If the durable property is set to true above, then a network-wide name must be defined so that a subscriber may be uniquely identified. This is used in conjunction with the clientID below.

clientID. Used in conjunction with the subscriber property above, it is used to uniquely identify a subscriber on the network.

Using the above method, both protocols were relatively easy to add with the SUBProtocol class containing 397 lines of code and the PUBProtocol class containing 363 lines. The helper classes SUBServer and PUBClient contain 238 and 168 lines of code respectively.

The above demonstrates that additional protocols may be added to RemoteJ without the parser needing to be extended to support the new protocol.

6.2.3   Testing and Evaluation

To test our implementation, we created two simple, although representative, classes, Publisher and Subscriber illustrated in Figure 6.2 and Figure 6.3 respectively.

Our Publisher class simply calls the publish() method passing it a String value and the Subscriber class calls the subscribe() method in a loop to demonstrate that it may be called by multiple clients.

Applying the DDL illustrated in Figure 6.4 allows the subscribe() method in the Subscriber class to asynchronously receive an event in the form of a string published on the REMOTEJ.SEND topic.

The topic is also defined as *durable* so that the event will be delivered when the subscriber application becomes available, if the event is published when the subscriber is unavailable.

```
public class Publisher {
    public static void main(String[] args) {
        Publisher a = new Publisher();
        a.publish("This is a test String \ldots{}");
        System.exit(0);
    }

    public void publish(String s) {
    }
}
```

FIGURE 6.2. Java Publisher class.

```
public class Subscriber {
    public static void main(String[] args) throws InterruptedException {
        Subscriber a = new Subscriber();
        while (true) {
            a.subscribe("This is not from the producer");
            Thread.sleep(5000);
        }
    }

    public void subscribe(String message) {
        System.out.println("Received: " + message);
    }
}
```

FIGURE 6.3. Java Subscriber class.

The `Publisher` class is altered so that calls to its `publish()` method are altered to send the `String` parameter as a message on the `REMOTEJ.SEND` topic. As can be seen in Figure 6.2 and Figure 6.3, the existing code is unaware of the protocol or recovery scenario that will be applied to it.

Running the applications verifies that the test applications work as expected with the `Publisher.publish()` method sending `String` objects that are received by the `Subscriber.subscribe()` method asynchronously.

6.2.4   Summary

In this section we have evaluated the extendibility of the RemoteJ system by adding two additional protocols, `pub` and `sub`. In contrast to the RMI, REST and JMS protocols, the `sub` protocol is event-driven as it alters the matched method to receive data asynchronously. The `pub` protocol alters the matched method to send its parameter as a message on a topic.

Both protocols are asynchronous and loosely-coupled in nature and are therefore decoupled in *time*, *space* and *synchronisation*, and our evaluation has demon-

```
import javax.jms.*;
import com.paul.*;

service Subscribe {
    protocol : sub {
     options {
        initialContextFactory =
           "org.apache.activemq.jndi.ActiveMQInitialContextFactory";
        topic = "REMOTEJ.SEND";
        durable = true;
        subscriber = "com.paul.PAUL";
        clientID = "sub";
        servers = "tcp://localhost:61616";
     }

     pointcut String Subscriber.subscribe() {
        recovery = nextServer;
     }
    }

    protocol : pub {
     options {
        initialContextFactory =
           "org.apache.activemq.jndi.ActiveMQInitialContextFactory";
        topic = "REMOTEJ.SEND";
        servers = "tcp://localhost:61616";
     }

     pointcut void Publisher.publish(String) {
        recovery = nextServer;
     }
    }
}
```

FIGURE 6.4. DDL for the publish/subscribe testing application. We define a DDL with both the pub and sub protocols in the same file. Upon compilation, both protocols are applied to their matching pointcuts.

strated that the RemoteJ and DDL concepts can be used for both synchronous tightly-coupled distributed systems as well as loosely-coupled asynchronous ones.

6.3   Evaluating Distributed Application Development in RemoteJ

This section evaluates the RemoteJ compiler/generator and DDL by converting a number of applications into distributed applications, using the framework ap-

```
public class Bank {
    private double balance;
    public BankServer() {
    }
    public void debit(double amount) {
        balance -= amount;
    }
    public void credit(double amount) {
        balance += amount;
    }
    public void create() {
        balance = 0;
    }
    public void open() {
        // open balance file
    }
    public void close() {
        // close balance file
    }
    public double getBalance() {
        return balance;
    }
}
```

FIGURE 6.5. Bank class.

proach for the RMI, REST and JMS protocols and then converting them using the RemoteJ compiler/generator and associated DDL files.

6.3.1   Bank Example

In this section we define a simple bank application and convert it to a distributed application using the RMI protocol. We then convert it using the RemoteJ compiler/generator and compare the different approaches.

Our bank application consists of the single class, **Bank**, illustrated in Figure 6.5. The class consists of six methods that we wish to make remote using the RMI protocol.

To convert the above application into an RMI application, we firstly need to define an interface containing the remote methods we wish to define as distributed.

We then alter the **Bank** class to extend the **UnicastRemoteObject** class and implement the **IBank** interface. Our converted class and interface is illustrated in Figure 6.6 on the left-hand side with the shaded areas illustrating the changes that needed to be made to the class to implement the RMI protocol. Note that in order to illustrate the requirements for exporting the remote object to the RMI registry we have added a **main** method.

As can be seen from the example, the RMI protocol requires developer's to adhere to both a coding convention as well as a framework. The methods

RMI Code	RemoteJ DDL

```
public class Bank extends UnicastRemoteObject
        implements IBank {
  private double balance;

  public Bank() throws RemoteException { }

  public static void main(String[] args) {
    if (System.getSecurityManager() == null) {
      System.setSecurityManager(
        new RMISecurityManager());
    }
    try {
      Bank obj = new Bank();
      Naming.rebind("//localhost/Bank", obj);
    } catch (Exception e) {
      e.printStackTrace();
    }
  }
  public void debit(double amount)
        throws RemoteException {
    balance -= amount;
  }
  public void credit(double amount)
        throws RemoteException {
    balance += amount;
  }
  public void create()
        throws RemoteException {
    balance = 0;
  }
  public void open()
        throws RemoteException {
    // open balance file
  }
  public void close()
        throws RemoteException {
    // close balance file
  }
  public double getBalance()
        throws RemoteException {
    return balance;
  }
}

public interface IBank extends Remote {
  public void debit(double amount)
    throws RemoteException;
  public void credit(double amount)
    throws RemoteException;
  public void create()
    throws RemoteException;
  public void open()
    throws RemoteException;
  public void close()
    throws RemoteException;
  public double getBalance()
    throws RemoteException;
}
```

```
import java.rmi.*;
import evaluation.bank.*;

service BankService {

  protocol : rmi {
    options {
        registryName = "RMITestServer";
        registryHost = "localhost";
        registryPort = 1099;
        hosts = "localhost,bookworm,bookpro";
        runEmbeddedRegistry = true;
    }

    pointcut void Bank.debit(double) {
      recovery = nextServer;
    }
    pointcut void Bank.credit(double) {
      recovery = nextServer;
    }
    pointcut void Bank.create() {
      recovery = nextServer;
    }
    pointcut void Bank.open() {
      recovery = nextServer;
    }
    pointcut void Bank.close() {
      recovery = nextServer;
    }
    pointcut double Bank.getBalance() {
      recovery = nextServer;
    }
  }
}
```

FIGURE 6.6. The Bank class converted to implement the RMI protocol on the left with the DDL that is required to provide the same functionality on the right.

that are to be exported must be defined in an interface that extends the Remote interface and the class where the methods are defined must implement the interface. All methods in the interface and the class must be declared to throw the RemoteException exception.

It should be noted that this example contains no recovery code.

```
service Desktop {

  protocol : rest {
    options {
      servers = "http://localhost";
      serverPort = 61616;
      serverThreads = 5;
    }
    pointcut void Server.updateData(Object) {
      recovery = abort;
    }
    pointcut void Server.stopViewer(InetAddress) {
      recovery = abort;
    }
    pointcut void Server.startViewer(InetAddress) {
      recovery = abort;
    }
    pointcut byte[] Server.getScreenCapture(InetAddress) {
      recovery = abort;
    }
    pointcut Rectangle Server.getScreenRect(InetAddress) {
      recovery = abort;
    }
  }
}
```

FIGURE 6.7. Java Remote Desktop REST DDL protocol file.

To convert the Bank class using the DDL requires the DDL file illustrated on the right-hand side of Figure 6.6, which generates both client and server code as well as the round-robin recovery scenario defined by the nextServer statement. The original Bank class is left unaltered and may be used to test a non-distributed version of the application or reused in another application.

6.3.2   Remote Desktop Example

Java Remote Desktop [1] is an open source project that provides a means of viewing and controlling a remote desktop via a GUI. A Swing client GUI communicates to a server-side component using the RMI protocol. The application supports any number of viewers and any changes performed in a client GUI screen is reflected in the other screens.

To evaluate RemoteJ, we firstly refactored the application to remove the RMI specific code. We then used RemoteJ to convert the now non-distributed application into a REST distributed application using the DDL illustrated in Figure 6.7.

To further test RemoteJ, we converted the same application into a JMS distributed application using the DDL in Figure 6.8.

```
service Desktop {

  protocol : jms {
    options {
      initialContextFactory =
        "org.apache.activemq.jndi.ActiveMQInitialContextFactory";
      persist = true;
      sendQueue = "REMOTEJ.SEND";
      receiveQueue = "temporary";
      servers = "tcp://localhost:61616,tcp://bookworm:61616";
      serverThreads = 5;
      receiveTimeout = 5000;
    }
    pointcut void Server.updateData(Object) {
      recovery = abort;
    }
    pointcut void Server.stopViewer(InetAddress) {
      recovery = abort;
    }
    pointcut void Server.startViewer(InetAddress) {
      recovery = abort;
    }
    pointcut byte[] Server.getScreenCapture(InetAddress) {
      recovery = abort;
    }
    pointcut Rectangle Server.getScreenRect(InetAddress) {
      recovery = abort;
    }
  }
}
```

FIGURE 6.8. Java Remote Desktop JMS protocol DDL file.

TABLE 6.1. Remote desktop LOC comparison.

	Original	*RemoteJ*	*% Difference*
LOC – JMS	1556	1431	8.03
LOC – REST	1556	1427	8.29
Number of Classes	12	9	25

As well as successfully being able to convert and run the Java remote desktop application, we were also, by removing the distribution concern, able to greatly simplify the application as illustrated in Table 6.1 where, using the JMS protocol, the number of lines of code was reduced by 8.03% and, using the REST protocol, by 8.29%. In addition, the number of classes was reduced from 12 to 9, a 25% reduction.

6.3.3 Other Applications

We have converted a number of other smaller applications to test RemoteJ, which we discuss below.

6.3.3.1 JClock

JClock is a simple application that displays the time in a GUI window and is supplied as part of the Java development kit. We successfully converted the application into a distributed application using both the RMI and JMS protocols.

The DDL for the JMS DDL is illustrated in Figure 5.8 and the RMI DDL in Figure 5.6.

In order to convert the JClock application into a distributed application we found it necessary to refactor the code to expose a method, `getDate()`, to retrieve the current system date. During the refactoring exercise we found that JClock starts a thread in its constructor, which resulted in the thread being started in both the client and server processes after being converted to a distributed application.

We believe this supports our assertion that it is necessary to ensure that applications that are to be distributed are developed with distribution in mind.

6.3.3.2 JShell

The JShell application [10] provides a UNIX style command shell written in Java. For our evaluation we converted it into a distributed application with the client portion prompting the user for a command and passing the command to the server for execution. The application was successfully converted using the JMS, RMI and REST protocols.

The DDL for the RMI DDL is illustrated in Figure 6.9, the JMS protocol in Figure 6.10 and the REST protocol in Figure 6.11.

We then further refactored the application to expose join points at a finer level of granularity to evaluate the DDL's scalability. The DDL for the further refactored JShell application using the RMI protocol is illustrated in Figure 6.12.

6.3.4 Summary

In this section we have evaluated the RemoteJ compiler/generator and the DDL. We have converted a number of applications into distributed applications using the RMI, JMS and REST protocols interchangeably without the underlying application code being aware of the distribution protocol or the recovery scenario.

This demonstrates that applications can be converted into distributed applications by the RemoteJ compiler/generator using any protocol and recovery scenario supported by the DDL.

```
import java.rmi.*;
import jshell.*;
import jshell.commandline.*;

service JShell {
    protocol : rmi {
      options {
          registryName = "RMIJShellServer";
          registryHost = "localhost";
          registryPort = 1099;
          runEmbeddedRegistry = true;
          serverPlugin = "com.paul.ServerPlugin";
      }

      pointcut String JShell.process_command_line(String) {}
    }
}
```

FIGURE 6.9. JShell RMI protocol DDL file.

```
import javax.jms.*;
import jshell.*;
import jshell.commandline.*;

service JShell {
    protocol : jms {
      options {
          destinationClass = "org.apache.activemq.command.ActiveMQQueue";
          initialContextFactory =
              "org.apache.activemq.jndi.ActiveMQInitialContextFactory";
          persist = true;
          sendQueue = "REMOTEJ.SEND";
          receiveQueue = "temporary"; // or name e.\,g. REMOTEJ.RECEIVE
          servers = "tcp://localhost:61616,tcp://bookworm:61616";
          serverThreads = 5;
          receiveTimeout = 5000;
          serverPlugin = "com.paul.ServerPlugin";
      }

      pointcut String JShell.process_command_line(String) {}
    }
}
```

FIGURE 6.10. JShell JMS protocol DDL file.

```
import javax.jms.*;
import jshell.*;
import jshell.commandline.*;

service JShell {

    protocol : rest {
     options {
        servers = "http://localhost";
        serverPort = 61616;
        serverThreads = 5;
     }

     pointcut String JShell.process_command_line(String) {}
    }
}
```

FIGURE 6.11.   JShell REST protocol DDL file.

6.4   Recovery Evaluation

As discussed in Section 5.3, RemoteJ supports four recovery scenarios, the `abort`, `continue` and `nextServer` statements as well as a user-defined recovery routine. The `abort` statement terminates the application in the event of an error while the `continue` statement simply ignores the error. Due to their simplicity, we do not consider these statements in our evaluation and instead concentrate on the `nextServer` statement and user-defined recovery routines.

6.4.1   Automatic Recovery

The `nextServer` statement simply cycles through a list of servers either declared in the DDL's `servers` statement or via the `remotej.servers` property. This allows for a simple recovery scenario where services are run on a number of machines in a network and in the event of a failure the client automatically reconnects to the next server in the list as illustrated in Figure 6.13.

If no servers can be contacted the application will be terminated as this is considered an unrecoverable error. If a server is successfully contacted following a previous failure, then knowledge of previous failures are discarded thereby allowing for the possibility that unavailable servers may become available.

For our evaluation we used the client code in Figure 6.14 and the associated DDL in Figure 6.15 to generate an RMI client and associated server. As can be seen in the client code, the test application simply calls the server repeatedly in a loop to obtain the current date. Although this is a simplistic example it adequately demonstrates the `nextServer` recovery capability.

```
import java.rmi.*;
import jshell.*;
import jshell.commandline.*;
import jshell.command.*;

service JShell {

    recovery RMIError (RemoteException e) {
        System.out.println("Got a RMI exception: " + e.getMessage());
        System.out.println("Method: " + transfer.getMethod());
        System.out.println("Host: " + transfer.getCurrentHost());
        System.out.println("Terminating application \ldots{}");
        System.exit(1);
    }

    protocol : rmi {
     options {
        registryName = "RMIJShellServer";
        registryHost = "localhost";
        registryPort = 1099;
        runEmbeddedRegistry = true;
     }

     pointcut String JShell.process_command_line(String) {
        recovery = RMIError;
     }

     pointcut void ls.execute(String[]) {}
     pointcut void ls.usage() {}
     pointcut void ls.process_environment() {}
     pointcut void ls.process_args(String[]) {}
     pointcut void ls.process_flag(String) {}
     pointcut void ls.add_files_in_current_directory() {}
     pointcut Vector ls.files() {}
     pointcut void ls.add_files_in_directory
        (File, Queue) {}
     pointcut void ls.sort_files(File[]) {}
     pointcut void ls.print_files(File[]) {}
     pointcut void ls.print_brief(File) {}
     pointcut void ls.print_detailed(File) {}
     pointcut void ls.print_remainder() {}
     pointcut void ls.pad(StringBuffer, int) {}
    }
}
```

FIGURE 6.12. Finer-grained JShell RMI protocol DDL file.

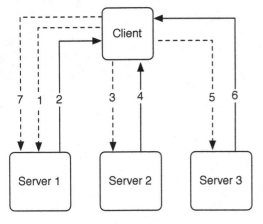

Calls: ----->
Response: ----->

1: Call getDate()
2. Call failed, call nextServer
3. Connect to Server 2
4. Call failed, call nextServer
5. Connect to Server 3
6. Call failed, call nextServer
7. Unrecoverable error if no servers have responded otherwise connect to Server 1.

FIGURE 6.13. Automatic recovery capability. The nextServer statement provides a simple clustering capability where a client request is redirected to an alternate server in the event of a distribution or communication error. If no servers can be contacted the application will be automatically terminated.

```java
public class ClockDate {

    public Date getDate() {
        return new Date();
    }

    public static void main(String[] args) throws InterruptedException {
        ClockDate cd = new ClockDate();
        while (true) {
            System.out.println("Current Date: " + cd.getDate());
            Thread.sleep(2000);
        }
    }
}
```

FIGURE 6.14. ClockDate class.

We began the evaluation by running the server-side application on three machines in a cluster and starting the client, which connected to the first server, localhost.

We aborted the first server, which caused the client to automatically reconnect to the next server, bookworm. We then restarted the first server and terminated the second thereby causing the client to automatically reconnect to the third server, bookpro.

```
import java.rmi.*;
import clock.*;

service ClockService {

  protocol : rmi {
    options {
        registryName = "RMITestServer";
        registryHost = "localhost";
        registryPort = 1099;
        runEmbeddedRegistry = true;
        servers = "localhost,bookworm,bookpro";
      }

      pointcut Date ClockDate.getDate () {
        recovery = nextServer;
      }
  }
}
```

FIGURE 6.15. RMI ClockService DDL for recovery testing.

After terminating the third server, the client reconnected to the first server again. We then terminated the first server which caused the application to abort with an error indicating that no servers were available thereby verifying correct operation of the `nextServer` statement.

Through this evaluation we were able to determine that a simple round-robin type of recovery routine could be correctly implemented in the DDL for all protocols, thereby removing the recovery concern from the client code and greatly simplifying the development of this type of recovery.

6.4.2   User-Defined Recovery Routines

The `nextServer` statement above provides useful recovery functionality for a class of applications running on a cluster of *known hosts*. While this may be sufficient for a large number of application types, it cannot be used in the scenario where servers, some of which are unknown at the time the application is started, leave and join the network over extended periods of time.

Although we could support this scenario in the RemoteJ code generator, with an associated DDL statement, we have chosen to implement it using a user-defined recovery routine so that we may evaluate the functionality and extendibility of RemoteJ's recovery system.

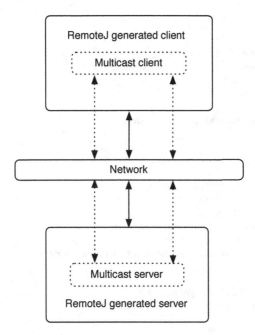

FIGURE 6.16. Multicast recovery. A multicast server is embedded
in the RemoteJ generated server using the `serverPlugin` statement, which allows the embedded code to run in a separate thread
in the server application. A user-defined recovery routine is then
able to interact with the server thread.

For our evaluation we implemented a simple system where a client in need
of an alternative server broadcasts a request on a multicast network[1]. The first
responding server, providing it is not the current server, is chosen.

For our implementation we embedded a simple multicast server in the RemoteJ generated server using RemoteJ's `serverPlugin` capability, described in
Section 5.3. Upon application startup, the `MulticastServer` server plugin is
started in a separate thread and waits for a broadcast on a well-known multicast
group and associated port number whose configuration may be changed by altering
the following property items for both the client and the server:

- `remotej.multicast.sendPort`. The port used to send the request on[2].
- `remotej.multicast.receivePort`. The port used to wait for a response.

---

[1] A multicast message is a message that is sent to a group of hosts that subscribe to an address
group, thereby allowing broadcasts to be sent to that group only rather than to an entire network.
Address groups are defined in the range 224.0.0.0 through 239.255.255.255 for the IP protocol
[96].
[2] Note that the client send port must equal the server receive port and the client receive port
must equal the server send port.

```
service ClockService {

  recovery Error (RemoteException e) {
    MulticastClient client = new MulticastClient();
    String[] s = new String[1];
    s[0] = client.getNextHost();
    setHosts(s);
    System.out.println("Switching to: " + s[0]);
  }

  protocol : rmi {
    options {
        registryName = "RMITestServer";
        registryHost = "localhost";
        registryPort = 1099;
        hosts = "localhost,bookworm,bookpro";
        runEmbeddedRegistry = true;
        serverPlugin = "uk.ac.glam.recovery.MulticastServer";
    }

    pointcut Date ClockDate.getDate () {
      recovery = Error;
    }
  }
}
```

FIGURE 6.17. RMI ClockService DDL for multicast recovery.

- `remoteJ.multicast.group`. The multicast group address.
- `remoteJ.multicast.ttl`. The time-to-live value. This value is used by routers to decide whether to pass the multicast datagram on to a destination network or not.

Our DDL, illustrated in Figure 6.17, sets the server plugin to our simple multicast server and uses a user-defined class, `MulticastClient`, in the recovery routine.

In the event of an error, the recovery routine creates an instance of the `MulticastClient` class and calls its `getNextHost()` method, which broadcasts a message on the network and waits for a response from a server process. Upon receipt of a response, the client sets the current host to the responding server's address and execution continues.

This recovery scenario and the interaction between client and server is illustrated in Figure 6.16.

6.4.3 Summary

The `nextServer` round-robin recovery routine provides a simple method of error recovery for a large proportion of applications. In the event of an error, the next server in the list of servers is used as the current server and a failure in all servers called in sequence (that is calling all servers in the list and receiving an error or no response from all of them) causes the application to terminate, thus avoiding an endless loop.

While this provides a simple and effective recovery scenario for many classes of applications, it cannot support the scenario where server processes come and go on the network – i.e. the *spontaneous network model* [117]. To support this model, and to evaluate the extendibility of RemoteJ's recovery capability, we have developed a server plugin and associated client class which is called directly from a user-defined recovery routine allowing a new server to be selected using a multicast technique.

This has demonstrated that RemoteJ's recovery model can be extended to support sophisticated recovery scenarios without the client code being aware of the recovery mechanism and yet still be able to participate in recovery scenarios.

6.5 Chapter Summary

The main goal of this project was to provide a contribution to the vision of autonomic computing and to simplify the development of distributed applications by modularising the distribution and recovery concerns and applying them to existing applications using a high-level domain-specific aspect language approach. As we have demonstrated a number of protocol implementations, using different distributed systems concepts, and have demonstrated the flexibility of the recovery concern, we believe we have succeeded with this goal.

Any claim to having provided an entirely new method of distributed systems development that can replace current methods cannot be made until RemoteJ's deficiencies are addressed and it can be tested and studied in a commercial environment. We discuss these deficiencies and future work in the next chapter.

Autonomics Development: A Domain-Specific Aspect Language Approach, 117–122
Book Series: Autonomic Systems
© 2010 Springer Basel AG

7 Conclusions and Future Work

7.1 Introduction

Our hypothesis statement declares that the distribution and recovery concerns can be completely and effectively modularised by defining them in a high-level domain-specific aspect language which can be applied to existing applications using a compiler/generator tool. We believe we have proven this hypothesis by the four contributions we have presented in this book. To recapitulate these are:

1. The concept of a Distribution Definition Language used to define classes and associated methods to be made distributed, the distributed system to use to make them distributed, and the recovery mechanism to use in the event of an error.
2. A simplified approach to the development of distributed systems that allows an existing application to be distributed, thereby improving software reusability and simplifying testability of distributed applications as applications may be functionally tested before having the distribution and recovery concerns applied.
3. The ability to apply one of a number of protocols to the same code base thereby generalising the distribution concern.
4. The application of distribution awareness to applications in such a way that the application is oblivious to the distribution implementation and recovery mechanism is yet able to fully participate in both.

We have evaluated and validated our approach by:

- Providing a case study of the addition of a publish/subscribe event-driven protocol to RemoteJ, which uses a different paradigm to the client-server model provided by the REST, RMI and the JMS request/reply protocols. These protocols were added without changes needing to be made to the DDL.
- Comparing the development of a number of simple distributed applications, developed using the RMI, REST and JMS protocols, with the RemoteJ approach. This has demonstrated that our approach allows multiple protocols to be applied to the same code base, thereby improving software reuse and testability by allowing applications to be tested for functional correctness before the distribution and recovery concerns are applied.
- Providing case studies of RemoteJ's recovery approach and evaluating it in terms of extendibility, flexibility and the ability to add the recovery concern

to existing applications. We provided a case study of extending the recovery capability by the use of user-defined recovery routines to provide a fairly sophisticated recovery scenario using network multicasting.

The main motivation of this project has been to simplify the development of distributed applications. We believe, by providing the above contributions, we have succeeded. However, as with many projects, further work needs to be done.

We have faced a number of challenges during the project that has led us to take various design decisions. We describe these challenges and decisions in Section 7.2. Areas for additional work are discussed in Section 7.3 and we present our conclusions in Section 7.4.

7.2   Challenges and Design Decisions

In this section we describe a number of challenges we have experienced and design decisions we have taken during this project.

7.2.1   Compiler/Generator

One of the early decisions of the project was whether to use a parser generator tool, such as ANTLR [81], for the compiler/generator or to develop our own parser generator. Faced with the prospect of hand-coding our own parser generator led us to evaluate the ANTLR tool. However we found that in order to use it we would have to extend the Java grammar as we allow Java statements in the DDL **recovery** statement. As the DDL is relatively simple we decided to adopt the compiler patterns defined by Watt and Brown [119] instead. As the addition of new protocols to the DDL can be done without extending the DDL grammar, as discussed in Section 6.2, this has proven to be the correct decision, as it would be difficult, or perhaps impossible, to provide this functionality using a parser generator tool.

7.2.2   Language Features

One of the fundamental challenges we were faced with during the design of the DDL was what to include and what not to include in the language. Our main desire was to keep the language as simple and elegant as possible yet be able to fully express the distribution and recovery concerns.

Our principle of ensuring that applications have been written with distribution in mind has been the guiding principle of our approach and has influenced many design decisions. This approach was adopted from the Waldo et al. [118] network awareness model. However, our implementation is fundamentally different as it removes the distribution and recovery concerns from the application's code, whereas the Waldo et al. [118] implementation tangles the distribution and recovery concepts in the application's code.

We believe this principle to be sound as the alternative, an automatic partitioning system, is complex to implement and, as shown by Tilevich [110], cannot work in all circumstances.

This approach has led us to not address concurrency because to do so would result in a distributed thread management system, a feature of an automatic partitioning system, which is outside the scope of our approach.

Initial versions of the DDL allowed the use of before, after and around advice in the `pointcut` statement. However, upon reflection, we decided to remove these statements as they added complexity to the language with little benefit, bearing in mind our primary principle.

The `plugin` statement, discussed in Section 6.4.2 provides an extension capability where used-defined code may be added to the DDL and accessed by the recovery routines. Although this is designed as an extension mechanism, common routines should be added to the DDL language instead. Exactly what to add will become clearer once RemoteJ can be tested and studied further.

7.2.3   Protocol Implementations

Adding the event-driven protocols, described in Section 6.2.1, resulted in a compromise having to be made in how the DDL is used, as the asynchronous protocols have a different usage model to the synchronous protocols. As discussed in Section 6.2.1, the use of the asynchronous protocols constrains the usage of the DDL as follows:

- DDL statements must match a single class/method.
- Methods matched by the pointcut statement must have a single serializable parameter that is either sent to the subscriber or received from the producer.
- Methods matched by the pointcut statement must be declared as returning `void`.

Although the above results in a different usage model depending on whether the protocol is synchronous or asynchronous, we believe that it is better than the alternative, which is different DDL statements for different models.

7.3   Future Work

The Distribution Definition Language currently has a number of shortcomings that should be addressed. We have identified the following areas for further research.

7.3.1   Parameters and Return Values

The DDL currently supports copy-by-value for parameters and return values. This could be extended to include pass-by-reference by adding a DDL statement `ref` (for reference) that may be applied to a parameter. For example:

> **pointcut** void ls.pad(**ref** StringBuffer, int) {}

declares that the `StringBuffer` parameter should be passed by reference.

While adding support for pass-by-reference in the DDL is fairly trivial, an implementation for all protocols, particularly those that don't support pass-by-reference, is not, as it requires a mechanism to call from the server to the client. For example, in the above pointcut, method calls on the `StringBuffer` class will result in a remote call from the server to the client to access the `StringBuffer` method called.

Although pass-by-reference is supported by some protocols, specifically RMI, it is not supported by all protocols. In order to implement pass-by-reference for all protocols, we believe it will be necessary to implement the callback mechanism described in Section 7.3.2 below.

The DDL does not currently support call-by-copy-restore as supported by J-Orchestra [111]. To support this an additional DDL keyword **restore** could be added to the DDL. For example:

> **pointcut** void ls.pad(**restore** StringBuffer, int) {}

declares that the `StringBuffer` parameter should be passed by call-by-copy-restore.

Again, extending the DDL to support call-by-copy-restore is fairly trivial although a method to implement it will require additional research.

7.3.2 Callback Support

The DDL does not currently support a callback mechanism to allow a server to call a remote object on the client or on another server.

There are a number of instances where callback support is useful. One is to support pass-by-reference for protocols that do not support it, as described above, and another is to support applications that need to call clients to update their current state.

An example of the latter is a distributed card game where a server sends its current state to all registered clients so that they may display the card selected by the server.

Another area for further research is to extend RemoteJ and the DDL to support servers that are clients to another server, possibly using a different protocol.

7.3.3 Recovery

The DDL does not currently support the management of exceptions that may occur on the server. For example, if a class file cannot be found or a database connection fails, it will result in the server failing with no notification to the client of the type of error that has occurred (besides that which may be supported by the protocol). These exceptions could be propagated back to the client and an application recovery capability, similar to the distribution recovery capability, could be added to the DDL to support application recovery.

Although not all application errors may be recoverable, the above examples can be if the server were to send the exception to the client and the client, using statements in the DDL, were to instruct the server to switch to another database server or to use a different URL for its CLASSSPATH.

This capability would greatly enhance the functionality of RemoteJ and simplify distributed application development further.

Our current recovery options include nextServer, abort, continue and user-defined recovery routines. As we have shown in Section 6.4.2, user-defined recovery routines can be used to provide fairly sophisticated recovery scenarios. However, the DDL should be extended to include a built-in multicast recovery facility similar to the one we developed in Section 6.4.2. We expect that as RemoteJ is further tested, and extended, additional recovery routines will be added to the DDL.

One of the primary candidates for an additional recovery mechanism is a stateful clustering capability. This would require the addition of a cluster recovery option to the DDL and the implementation could either be developed or existing clustering frameworks, such as Terracotta [3], may be embedded in RemoteJ.

7.3.4   Autonomic Features

Autonomics is primarily concerned with the development of systems that are able to manage themselves, given high-level objectives by administrators, so that they may adjust their operation, workloads, demands and external conditions in the face of hardware or software failures

The RemoteJ language, and in particular its support for the modularisation of the recovery concern, provides the ability for a distributed system to heal itself in the face of server failures by connecting to another server, if the current server should become unavailable, using one of a number of predefined methods or by the implementation of a new recovery method.

This approach allows autonomics development to be greatly simplified compared to current framework approaches and RemoteJ can be further extended to support other autonomic features, such as autonomic policies, autonomic sensors, the ability to monitor remote servers and automatically switch to the one with less latency and so forth. Dynamic support may be provided by embedding hooks into existing code to allow the dynamic replacement or extension of referenced classes using any framework supported by the DDL.

A domain-specific aspect language is a powerful concept that may be used as a general method to apply autonomic features to applications thereby greatly simplifying their development.

7.4   Conclusion

This book has presented four contributions to improving the development of distributed applications.

Firstly, we have introduced the concept of a *Distribution Definition Language*, a high-level domain-specific aspect language that generalises the distribution concern by describing the classes and methods of an existing application to be made remote, the distributed system to use to make them remote, and the recovery mechanism to use in the event of a remote error. Secondly, we provided the ability for multiple protocols to be applied to the same code base, thereby generalising the distribution concern. Thirdly, we allowed the application of distribution awareness to applications in such a way that the application is oblivious to the distribution implementation and recovery mechanism yet is able to fully participate in both. Finally, we provided a simplified approach to the development of distributed systems that allows an application to be either distributed or non-distributed, thereby improving software reuse and simplifying testability of distributed applications, as applications may be functionally tested before having the distribution and recovery concerns applied.

In addition, these contributions, by alleviating some of the complexity involved in distributed systems development and by allowing autonomic features, such as recovery, to be transparently added to existing applications, provides a contribution to autonomic computing. We propose that the concept of a domain-specific aspect language be used as a general method to apply autonomic frameworks, thereby greatly easing the programmers burden and ensuring correct use of the framework, which reduces the effort required to develop autonomic applications.

As with many projects of this kind, additional work is needed to improve and refine the concept further. Some of this work is currently underway and we look forward to addressing the other outstanding issues.

Autonomics Development: A Domain-Specific Aspect Language Approach, 123–124
Book Series: Autonomic Systems
© 2010 Springer Basel AG

Appendix A: RemoteJ Syntax

RemoteJService	::=	*(ImportNameList)* Service*
ImportNameList	::=	*SingleImport (SingleImport)**
SingleImport	::=	**import** *Imports Semi*
Imports	::=	*Identifier (Dot | Wildcard)**
Service	::=	**service** *Identifier LeftCurley StatementList RightCurley*
StatementList	::=	*(RecoverList)* (ProtocolList)+*
RecoveryList	::=	*RecoveryStatement (RecoveryStatement)**
RecoveryStatement	::=	**recovery** *RecoveryName LeftBracket ClassName Variable RightBracket LeftCurley JavaStatement RightCurley*
ProtocolList	::=	*ProtocolStatement (ProtocolStatement)**
ProtocolStatement	::=	**protocol** *Identifier Colon LeftCurley Options (PointcutStatement)+ RightCurley*
Options	::=	*(Identifier = Identifier)+*
PointcutStatement	::=	**pointcut** *ReturnValue PointcutName LeftBracket (((Parameter)? (Comma Parameter)*)	ParameterWildcard) RightBracket LeftCurley RecoveryType RightCurley*
ReturnValue	::=	*ClassName	PrimitiveType |* **void**
PointcutName	::=	*Identifier (Dot Identifier | Wildcard)**
Parameter	::=	*ClassName	PrimitiveType*

RecoveryType	::=	**recovery** *Equals RecoveryOption Semi*
RecoveryOption	::=	*RecoveryName* | **continue** | **abort** | **nextServer**
RecoveryName	::=	*Identifier*
ClassName	::=	*Identifier (Dot Identifier)**
PrimitiveType	::=	**boolean** | **byte** | **char** | **short** | **int** | **long** | **float** | **double**
Variable	::=	*Identifier*
JavaStatement	::=	*Any Java statement accepted by Javassist [19]*
Identifier	::=	*('a'..'z' | 'A'..'Z')+ (IntegerLiteral)**
IntegerLiteral	::=	*0..255*
Comma	::=	,
Semi	::=	;
Dot	::=	.
LeftCurly	::=	{
RightCurley	::=	}
LeftBracket	::=	(
RightBracket	::=	)
Colon	::=	:
Equals	::=	=
Wildcard	::=	*
ParameterWildcard	::=	..

References

[1] Java Remote Desktop [online]. 2008 [last accessed: 6 April 2008]. Available from: http://sourceforge.net/projects/jrdesktop/.

[2] Lightweight REST framework for Java [online]. 2008a [last accessed: 20 April 2008]. Available from: http://www.restlet.org/.

[3] Terracotta [online]. 2008b [last accessed: 21 April 2008]. Available from: http://www.terracotta.org/.

[4] Ananda, A. L., B. H. Tay, and E. K. Koh, A survey of asynchronous remote procedure calls, *ACM SIGOPS Operating Systems Review*, *26*(2), 92–109, 1992.

[5] Apache Software Foundtion, Apache ActiveMQ 4.0 Developer Guide, 2006. Available from: http://activemq.apache.org/developer-guide.html [last accessed: 25 February 2007].

[6] AspectJ Team, The AspectJ programming guide, 2004. Available from: http://eclipse.org/aspectj/doc/released/progguide [last accessed: 12 January 2007].

[7] Baker, S., *CORBA Distributed Objects*. Addison-Wesley, 1997.

[8] Bal, H. E., Orca: A Language for Distributed Programming, *SIGPLAN Notices*, *25*(5), 17–24, 1990.

[9] Banavar, G., T. D. Chandra, R. E. Strom, and D. C. Sturman, A case for message oriented middleware, in *Proceedings of the 13th International Symposium on Distributed Computing*, 1–18, London, UK. Springer-Verlag, 1999.

[10] Beard, P., JShell Project, 2001. Available from: http://homepage.mac.com/pcbeard/JShell [last accessed: 8 August 2007].

[11] Beck, K., and E. Gamma, Test-infected: programmers love writing tests, in *More Java gems*, 357–376. Cambridge University Press, New York, NY, USA, 2000.

[12] Bergmans, L., and M. Aksit, Composing crosscutting concerns using composition filters, *Communications of the ACM*, *44*(10), 51–57, 2001.

[13] Berners-Lee, T., Universal Resource Identifiers in WWW: A Unifying Syntax for the Expression of Names and Addresses of Objects on the Network as used in the World-Wide Web, RFC 1630 (Informational), 1994. Available from: http://www.ietf.org/rfc/rfc1630.txt [last accessed: 20 April 2008].

[14] Birrell, A., G. Nelson, S. Owicki, and E. Wobber, Network Objects, *Software Practice and Experience*, *25*(S4), 87–130, 1995.

[15] Birrell, A. D., and B. J. Nelson, Implementing remote procedure calls, *ACM Transactions on Computer Systems (TOCS)*, *2*(1), 39–59, 1984.

[16] Bonér, J., What are the key issues for commercial AOP use: how does AspectWerkz address them?, in *Proceedings of the 3rd International Conference on Aspect-Oriented Software Development*, Lancaster, UK. 2004.

[17] Bracha, G., and W. Cook, Mixin-based inheritance, in *Proceedings of the Conference on Object-Oriented Programming: Systems, Languages, and Applications / Proceedings of the European Conference on Object-Oriented Programming*, 303–311. ACM Press, 1990.

[18] Ceccato, M., and P. Tonella, Adding Distribution to Existing Applications by Means of Aspect Oriented Programming, in *Fourth IEEE International Workshop on Source Code Analysis and Manipulation*, 107–116, Washington, DC, USA. 2004.

[19] Chiba, S., and M. Nishizawa, An Easy-to-Use Toolkit for Efficient Java Bytecode Translators, in *Proceedings of the 2nd International Conference on Generative Programming and Component Engineering (GPCE '03)*, 364–376. Springer-Verlag, 2003.

[20] Coady, Y., G. Kiczales, M. Feeley, N. Hutchinson, and J. S. Ong, Structuring operating system aspects: using AOP to improve OS structure modularity, *Communications of the ACM*, *44*(10), 79–82, 2001.

[21] Constantinides, C., A. Bader, T. Elrad, P. Netinant, and M. E. Fayad, Designing an aspect-oriented framework in an object-oriented environment, *ACM Computing Surveys (CSUR)*, *32*(1es), 41, 2000.

[22] Cooper, E. C., Replicated procedure call, in *PODC '84: Proceedings of the Third Annual ACM Symposium on Principles of Distributed Computing*, 220–232, Vancouver, British Columbia, Canada. ACM Press, 1984.

[23] Coulouris, G. F., J. Dollimore, and T. Kindberg, *Distributed Systems: Concepts and Design*. Addison-Wesley, 4th edn., 2005.

[24] Deutsch, P., The Eight Fallacies of Distributed Computing, 1994. Available from: http://en.wikipedia.org/wiki/Fallacies_of_Distributed_Computing [last accessed: 5 August 2007].

[25] Dickman, A., *Designing Applications with MSMQ: Message Queuing for Developers*. Addison-Wesley Longman Publishing Co., Inc., Boston, MA, USA, 1998.

[26] Dineen, T. H., P. J. Leach, N. W. Mishkin, J. N. Pato, and G. L. Wyant, The Network Computing Architecture and System: An Environment for Developing Distributed Applications, in *Compcon Spring '88. Thirty-Third IEEE Computer Society International Conference*, San Francisco, CA, USA. 1988.

[27] Dogac, A., C. Dengi, and M. T. Öszu, Distributed object computing platforms, *Communications of the ACM*, (9), 95–103, 1998.

[28] Downing, T. B., *Java RMI: Remote Method Invocation*. IDG Books, 1998.

[29] Dronavalli, N., An Optimized Design For Multi-Protocol Communication Systems, Master's thesis, Rutgers University, 1998.

[30] Duzan, G., J. Loyall, R. Schantz, R. Shapiro, and J. Zinky, Building adaptive distributed applications with middleware and aspects, in *AOSD '04: Proceedings of the 3rd international conference on Aspect-oriented software development*, 66–73, New York, NY, USA. ACM, 2004.

[31] Elrad, T., M. Aksit, G. Kiczales, K. Lieberherr, and H. Ossher, Discussing aspects of AOP, *Communications of the ACM*, *44*(10), 33–38, 2001.

[32] Emmerich, W., M. Aoyama, and J. Sventek, The impact of research on middleware technology, *SIGOPS Operating Systems Review*, *41*(1), 89–112, 2007.

[33] Engel, M., and B. Freisleben, Supporting autonomic computing functionality via dynamic operating system kernel aspects, in *AOSD '05: Proceedings of the 4th international conference on Aspect-oriented software development*, 51–62, New York, NY, USA. ACM, 2005.

[34] Eugster, P. T., P. A. Felber, R. Guerraoui, and A.-M. Kermarrec, The many faces of publish/subscribe, *ACM Computing Surveys*, *35*(2), 114–131, 2003.

[35] Fabry, J., and T. D'Hondt, KALA: Kernel Aspect language for advanced transactions, in *Proceedings of the 2006 ACM Symposium on Applied Computing*, Dijon, France. ACM Press, 2006.

[36] Fayad, M. E., D. C. Schmidt, and R. E. Johnson, *Building Application Frameworks: Object-Oriented foundations of Framework Design*. John Wiley & Sons, Inc., 1999.

[37] Fielding, R., J. Gettys, J. Mogul, H. Frystyk, L. Masinter, P. Leach, and T. Berners-Lee, Hypertext Transfer Protocol – HTTP/1.1, 1999.

[38] Fielding, R. T., Architectural styles and the design of network-based software architectures, Ph.D. thesis, University of California, Irvine, 2000.

[39] Fielding, R. T., and R. N. Taylor, Principled design of the modern Web architecture, in *ICSE '00: Proceedings of the 22nd International Conference on Software Engineering*, 407–416, New York, NY, USA. ACM, 2000.

[40] Freeman, E., K. Arnold, and S. Hupfer, *JavaSpaces Principles, Patterns, and Practice*. Addison-Wesley Longman Ltd. Essex, UK, 1999.

[41] Gamma, E., R. Helm, R. E. Johnson, and J. Vissides, *Design Patterns. Elements of Reusable Object-Oriented Software*. Addison-Wesley, 1995.

[42] Goth, G., Critics Say Web Services Need a REST, *IEEE Distributed Systems Online*, 5(12), 1, 2004.

[43] Grace, P., E. Truyen, B. Lagaisse, and W. Joosen, The case for aspect-oriented reflective middleware, in *ARM '07: Proceedings of the 6th international workshop on Adaptive and reflective middleware*, 1–6, New York, NY, USA. ACM, 2007.

[44] Greenwood, P., and L. Blair, Using Dynamic Aspect-Oriented Programming to Implement an Autonomic System, in *Proceedings of the 2004 Dynamic Aspects Workshop (DAW04), Lancaster*, 76–88. 2004. Available from: http://www.comp.lancs.ac.uk/computing/aose/papers/dynFr_daw04.pdf.

[45] Greenwood, P., and L. Blair, A Framework for Policy Driven Auto-Adaptive Systems using Dynamic Framed Aspects, *Lecture Notes in Computer Science, 4242*, 30–65, 2006.

[46] Hanenberg, S., and R. Unland, Parametric introductions, in *Proceedings of the 2nd International Conference on Aspect-Oriented Software Development*, 80–89. Boston, Massachusetts, 2003.

[47] Hapner, M., R. Burridge, R. Sharma, J. Fialli, and K. Stout, Java Message Service, 2002. Available from: http://java.sun.com/products/jms/docs.html [last accessed: 20 October 2007].

[48] Heindel, L. E., and V. A. Kasten, Highly reliable synchronous and asynchronous remote procedure calls, in *Proceedings of the 1996 IEEE Fifteenth Annual International Phoenix Conference on Computers and Communications*, 103–107, Scottsdale, AZ, USA. IEEE, 1996.

[49] Hicks, M., S. Jagannathan, R. Kelsey, J. T. Moore, and C. Ungureanu, Transparent communication for distributed objects in Java, in *Proceedings of the ACM 1999 Conference on Java Grande*, 160–170. New York, NY, USA ACM Press, 1999.

[50] Hohpe, G., and B. Woolf, *Enterprise Integration Patterns: Designing, Building, and Deploying Messaging Solutions*. Addison-Wesley Professional, 2003.

[51] IBM Corporation, MQSeries: An introduction to messaging and queuing, Tech. Rep. GC33-0805-01, IBM Corporation, 1995. Available from: ftp://ftp.software.ibm.com/software/mqseries/pdf/horaa101.pdf [last accessed: 24 March 2008].

[52] IBM Corporation, Autonomic Computing: IBM's perspective on the State of Information Technology, 2001. Available from: http://www.research.ibm.com/autonomic/manifesto/autonomic_computing.pdf [last accessed: 6 January 2009].

[53] Interface21, *Spring Java/J2EE Application Framework 2.0*, 2007. Available from: http://static.springframework.org/spring/docs/2.0.x/spring-reference.pdf [last accessed: 1 October 2007].

[54] JBoss, *JBoss AOP - User Guide*, 2005. Available from: http://docs.jboss.com/aop/1.3/aspect-framework/userguide/en/html/index.html [last accessed: 20 January 2007].

[55] Johnson, R. E., and B. Foote, Designing Reusable Classes, *Journal of Object-Oriented Programming*, *1*(2), 22–35, 1988.

[56] Kephart, J. O., and D. M. Chess, The Vision of Autonomic Computing, *IEEE Computer*, *36*(1), 41–50, 2003.

[57] Khare, R., and R. N. Taylor, Extending the Representational State Transfer (REST) Architectural Style for Decentralized Systems, in *ICSE '04: Proceedings of the 26th International Conference on Software Engineering*, 428–437, Washington, DC, USA. IEEE Computer Society, 2004.

[58] Kiczales, G., and J. D. Rivieres, *The Art of the Metaobject Protocol*. MIT Press, Cambridge, MA, USA, 1991.

[59] Kiczales, G., J. Lamping, A. Menhdhekar, C. Maeda, C. Lopes, J.-M. Loingtier, and J. Irwin, Aspect-Oriented Programming, in *Proceedings of the European Conference on Object-Oriented Programming*, edited by M. Akşit, and S. Matsuoka, vol. 1241, 220–242, Berlin, Heidelberg, and New York. Springer-Verlag, 1997.

[60] Kiczales, G., E. Hilsdale, J. Hugunin, M. Kersten, J. Palm, and W. G. Griswold, An Overview of AspectJ, *Lecture Notes in Computer Science*, *2072*, 327–355, 2001a.

[61] Kiczales, G., E. Hilsdale, J. Hugunin, M. Kersten, J. Palm, and W. G. Griswold, Getting started with AspectJ, *Communications of the ACM*, *44*(10), 59–65, 2001b.

[62] Kurzyniec, D., T. Wrzosek, V. Sunderam, and A. Sominski, RMIX: A Multiprotocol RMI Framework for Java, in *IPDPS '03: Proceedings of the 17th International Symposium on Parallel and Distributed Processing*, 140, Washington, DC, USA. IEEE Computer Society, 2003.

[63] Lewis, J. A., S. M. Henry, D. G. Kafura, and R. S. Schulman, An empirical study of the object-oriented paradigm and software reuse, *ACM SIGPLAN Notices*, *26*(11), 184–196, 1991.

[64] Lieberherr, K., D. H. Lorenz, and M. Mezini, Programming with Aspectual Components, Tech. Rep. NU-CCS-99-01, College of Computer Science, Northeastern University, 1999.

[65] Lopes, C. V., D: A Language Framework for Distributed Programming, Ph.D. thesis, College of Computer Science, Northeastern University, 1997.

[66] Lopes, C. V., and G. Kiczales, D: A Language Framework for Distributed Programming, Tech. rep., Xerox Palo Alto Research Center, 1997.

[67] Maes, P., Concepts and experiments in computational reflection, in *OOPSLA '87: Conference proceedings on Object-oriented programming systems, languages and applications*, 147–155, New York, NY, USA. ACM, 1987.

[68] McDirmid, S., M. Flatt, and W. C. Hsieh, Jiazzi: New-Age Components for Old-Fashioned Java, in *Proceedings of the ACM Conference on Object-Oriented Programming, Systems, Languages, and Applications (OOPSLA)*, vol. (11) 36, 211–222. Tampa Florida USA, 2001.

[69] McKinley, P. K., S. M. Sadjadi, E. P. Kasten, and B. H. C. Cheng, Composing Adaptive Software, *IEEE Computer*, *37*(7), 56–64, 2004.

[70] Mendhekar, A., G. Kiczales, and J. Lamping, RG: A Case-Study for Aspect-Oriented Programming, Tech. Rep. SPL97-009 P9710044, Xerox Palo Alto Research Center, 1997.

[71] Mezini, M., and K. Ostermann, Conquering aspects with Caesar, in *Proceedings of the 2nd International Conference on Aspect-Oriented Software Development*, 90–99. Boston, Massachusetts, 2003.

[72] Munnelly, J., and S. Clarke, ALPH: A Domain-Specific Language for Crosscutting Pervasive Healthcare Concerns, in *Proceedings of the 2nd Workshop on Domain Specific Aspect Languages, AOSD '07*, Vancouver, British Columbia, Canada. ACM Press, 2007.

[73] Navarro, L. D. B., M. Südholt, W. Vanderperren, B. De Fraine, and D. Suvée, Explicitly distributed AOP using AWED, in *Proceedings of the 5th International Conference on Aspect-Oriented Software Development*, 51–62, Bonn, Germany. 2006.

[74] Nishizawa, M., S. Chiba, and M. Tatsubori, Remote pointcut: a language construct for distributed AOP, in *AOSD '04: Proceedings of the 3rd International Conference on Aspect-Oriented Software Development*, 7–15, Lancaster, UK. 2004.

[75] Object Management Group, *Common Object Request Broker Architecture: Core Specification*, Object Management Group, Needham, MA USA, 3.0.3 edn., 2004a. Available from: http://www.omg.org/docs/formal/04-03-12.pdf [last accessed: 16 July 2007].

[76] Object Management Group, *CORBA Event Service Specification*, Object Management Group, Needham, MA USA, 1.2 edn., 2004b. Available from: http://www.omg.org/docs/formal/04-10-02.pdf [last accessed: 12 March 2008].

[77] Object Management Group, *CORBA Component Model Specification, v4.0*, 2006. Available from: http://www.omg.org/docs/formal/06-04-01.pdf [last accessed: 16 July 2007].

[78] Oki, B., M. Pfluegl, A. Siegel, and D. Skeen, The Information Bus: an architecture for extensible distributed systems, in *SOSP '93: Proceedings of the Fourteenth ACM Symposium on Operating Systems Principles*, 58–68, New York, NY, USA. ACM, 1993.

[79] Ossher, H., and P. Tarr, Using multidimensional separation of concerns to (re)shape evolving software, *Communications of the ACM, 44*(10), 43–50, 2001.

[80] Pace, A. D., and M. Campo, Analyzing the role of aspects in software design, *Communications of the ACM, 44*(10), 66–73, 2001.

[81] Parr, T. J., and R. W. Quong, ANTLR: a predicated-LL(k) parser generator, *Software Practice and Experience, 25*(7), 789–810, 1995.

[82] Pawlak, R., L. Seinturier, L. Duchien, and G. Florin, JAC: A Flexible Solution for Aspect-Oriented Programming in Java, in *REFLECTION '01: Proceedings of the Third International Conference on Metalevel Architectures and Separation of Crosscutting Concerns*, 1–24, London, UK. Springer-Verlag, 2001.

[83] Philippsen, M., and M. Zenger, JavaParty - Transparent Remote Objects in Java, *Concurrency: Practice & Experience, 9*(11), 1225–1242, 1997.

[84] Popovici, A., G. Alonso, and T. Gross, Just-in-time aspects: efficient dynamic weaving for Java, in *Proceedings of the 2nd International Conference on Aspect-Oriented Software Development,*, 100–109, Boston, Massachusetts. 2003.

[85] Pree, W., Meta Patterns - A Means For Capturing the Essentials of Reusable Object-Oriented Design, in *ECOOP '94: Proceedings of the 8th European Conference on Object-Oriented Programming*, 150–162, London, UK. Springer-Verlag, 1994.

[86] Pree, W., *Design Patterns for Object-Oriented Software Development*. Addison-Wesley, Reading MA, 1995.

[87] Rosenblum, D. S., and A. L. Wolf, A design framework for Internet-scale event observation and notification, *SIGSOFT Software Engineering Notes*, *22*(6), 344–360, 1997.

[88] Schmidt, E., The Berkeley UNIX Network, Master's thesis, Berkeley, 1979.

[89] Sherman, M., Architecture of the Encina distributed transaction processing family, in *SIGMOD '93: Proceedings of the 1993 ACM SIGMOD International Conference on Management of Data*, 460–463, Washington, D.C., United States. ACM Press, 1993.

[90] Soares, P. G., On remote procedure call, in *CASCON '92: Proceedings of the 1992 Conference of the Centre for Advanced Studies on Collaborative Research*, 215–267, Toronto, Ontario, Canada. IBM Press, 1992.

[91] Soares, S., E. Laureano, and P. Borba, Implementing distribution and persistence aspects with AspectJ, in *OOPSLA '02: Proceedings of the 17th ACM SIGPLAN Conference on Object-Oriented Programming, Systems, Languages, and Applications*, 174–190, Seattle, Washington, USA. ACM Press, 2002.

[92] Soule, P., A Domain-Specific Aspect Language Approach to Distributed Systems Development, Ph.D. thesis, University of Glamorgan, Pontypridd Wales, United Kingdom, 2008.

[93] Soule, P., T. Carnduff, and S. Lewis, A Distribution Definition Language for the Automated Distribution of Java Objects, in *Proceedings of the 2nd workshop on Domain Specific Aspect Languages, AOSD '07*, Vancouver, British Columbia, Canada. ACM Press, 2007.

[94] Sousan, W., V. Winter, M. Zand, and H. Siy, ERTSAL: a prototype of a domain-specific aspect language for analysis of embedded real-time systems, in *Proceedings of the 2nd Workshop on Domain Specific Aspect Languages, AOSD '07*, Vancouver, British Columbia, Canada. ACM Press, 2007.

[95] Spector, A. Z., Performing remote operations efficiently on a local computer network, *Communications of the ACM*, *25*(4), 246–260, 1982.

[96] Stevens, W. R., *UNIX Network Programming*. Prentice Hall Software Series, 1st edn., 1990.

[97] Sun Microsystems, *RFC 1014 - XDR: External Data Representation Standard*, 1987. Available from: http://www.ietf.org/rfc/rfc1014.txt [last accessed: 17 December 2007].

[98] Sun Microsystems, *RFC 1050 - RPC: Remote Procedure Call Protocol Specification*, 1988. Available from: http://tools.ietf.org/html/rfc1831 [last accessed: 12 January 2007].

[99] Sun Microsystems, *NFS: Network File System Protocol Specification (RFC 1094)*, 1989. Available from: http://www.faqs.org/rfcs/rfc1094.html [last accessed: 16 July 2007].

[100] Sun Microsystems, *Java Naming and Directory Interface (JNDI)*, 1999. Available from: http://java.sun.com/products/jndi/docs.html [last accessed: 22 October 2007].

[101] Sun Microsystems, *Getting Started with Java IDL*, 2001a. Available from: http://java.sun.com/j2se/1.4.2/docs/guide/idl/GShome.html [last accessed: January 2008].

[102] Sun Microsystems, *Jini Technology Core Platform Specification*, 2001b. Available from: http://java.sun.com/products/jini/2_1index.html [last accessed: 20 October 2007].

[103] Sun Microsystems, *EJB 2.1 Specification*, 2003. Available from: http://java.sun.com/products/ejb/docs.html [last accessed: 12 January 2007].

[104] Sun Microsystems, *Enterprise JavaBeans Specification Version 3.0*, 2006. Available from: http://jcp.org/aboutJava/communityprocess/final/jsr220/index.html [last accessed: November 2007].

[105] Surajbali, B., G. Coulson, P. Greenwood, and P. Grace, Augmenting reflective middleware with an aspect orientation support layer, in *ARM '07: Proceedings of the 6th international workshop on Adaptive and reflective middleware*, 1–6, New York, NY, USA. ACM, 2007.

[106] Suvée, D., W. Vanderperren, and V. Jonckers, JAsCo: an Aspect-Oriented approach tailored for Component Based Software Development, in *Proceedings of the 2nd International Conference on Aspect-Oriented Software Development*, 21–29. 2003.

[107] Tanenbaum, A. S., Network protocols, *ACM Computing Surveys*, *13*(4), 453–489, 1981.

[108] Tay, B. H., and A. L. Ananda, A survey of remote procedure calls, *ACM SIGOPS Operating Systems Review*, *24*(3), pp. 68–79, 1990.

[109] The Open Group, *DCE 1.1: Remote Procedure Call*. The Open Group, 1997.

[110] Tilevich, E., Software Tools for Separating Distribution Concerns, Ph.D. thesis, College of Computing, Georgia Institute of Technology, 2005.

[111] Tilevich, E., and Y. Smaragdakis, NRMI: Natural and efficient middleware, in *Proceedings of the 23rd International Conference on Distributed Computing Systems*, 252–261. 2003.

[112] Tilevich, E., and Y. Smaragdakis, Portable and Efficient Distributed Threads for Java, in *ACM/IFIP/USENIX 5th International Middleware Conference (Middleware '04)*, Toronto, Ontario, Canada. 2004.

[113] Tilevich, E., and S. Urbanski, J-Orchestra: Automatic Java Application Partitioning, in *European Conference on Object-Oriented Programming (ECOOP)*, Malaga. 2002.

[114] Tilevich, E., S. Urbanski, Y. Smaragdakis, and M. Fleury, Aspectizing Server-Side Distribution, in *21st IEEE/ACM International Conference on Automated Software Engineering*, Tokyo, Japan. 2003.

[115] Vogels, W., Web services are not distributed objects, *IEEE Internet computing*, 7(6), 59–66, 2003.

[116] Waldo, J., Remote procedure calls and Java Remote Method Invocation, *IEEE Concurrency*, 6(3), 5–7, 1998.

[117] Waldo, J., The Jini architecture for network-centric computing, *Communications of the ACM*, 42(7), 76–82, 1999.

[118] Waldo, J., G. Wyant, A. Wollrath, and S. Kendall, A Note on Distributed Computing, Tech. rep., Sun Microsystems, 1994. Available from: http://research.sun.com/techrep/1994/smli_tr-94-29.pdf [last accessed: 12 January 2007].

[119] Watt, D., and D. Brown, *Programming Language Processors in Java: Compilers and Interpreters*. Prentice Hall, 2000.

[120] Weiser, M., The computer for the twenty-first century, *Scientific American*, 94–104, 1991.

[121] White, J., Simplifying Autonomic Enterprise Java Bean Applications via Model-driven Development: a Case Study, in *The Journal of Software and System Modeling*, 601–615. 2005.

[122] Wollrath, A., J. Waldo, and R. Riggs, Java-centric distributed computing, *IEEE Micro*, 17(3), 44–53, 1997.